COMPANY PRODUCTIVITY

MEASUREMENT FOR IMPROVEMENT

IRVING H. SIEGEL

April 1980

THE W. E. UPJOHN INSTITUTE FOR EMPLOYMENT RESEARCH

Library of Congress Cataloging in Publication Data

Siegel, Irving Herbert.
  Company productivity.

  1. Industrial productivity—Measurement.
I. Title.
HD56.S48   658.5'036   80-11930
ISBN 0-911558-60-8 (pbk.)

THE INSTITUTE, a nonprofit research organization, was established on July 1, 1945. It is an activity of the W. E. Upjohn Unemployment Trustee Corporation, which was formed in 1932 to administer a fund set aside by the late Dr. W. E. Upjohn for the purpose of carrying on "research into the causes and effects of unemployment and measures for the alleviation of unemployment."

The Author

Irving H. Siegel, a consulting economist, received his Ph.D. from Columbia University. His doctoral dissertation, "Concepts and Measurement of Production and Productivity," was reproduced by the Bureau of Labor Statistics as a working paper for a national productivity conference in 1952 and was widely used by researchers and educators in many countries for almost another decade. Dr. Siegel has been associated with Johns Hopkins University Operations Research Office, the Twentieth Century Fund, and the National Bureau of Economic Research. His government service has included chief economist of the Veterans Administration, member of the economic staff of the President's Council of Economic Advisers, and economic advisor to the Bureau of Domestic Business Development in the Department of Commerce. He is a fellow of the American Statistical Association, the American Association for the Advancement of Science, and the New York Academy of Sciences.

Go, little book, endowed with separate self
To serve—not stand and wait upon a shelf.

Foreword

The W. E. Upjohn Institute is pleased to sponsor this publication by Dr. Irving H. Siegel, who comes to his subject with long experience and unique credentials. The need for signal improvement in the national rate of productivity advance is unarguable. Such improvement is an essential element of efforts designed to counter inflation and preserve jobs and the American living standard.

If, as the author maintains, organizations can inexpensively quicken their own productivity pace by means of productivity measurement, this monograph could make a solid contribution to the national interest. With this potential in view, the Institute is eager to secure a wide readership among business executives and managers, government officials, and the various professionals upon whom they will have to rely for translation of the potential into a reality.

Facts and observations presented in this monograph are the sole responsibility of the author. His viewpoints do not necessarily represent positions of the W. E. Upjohn Institute for Employment Research.

E. Earl Wright
Director

Preface

This monograph is largely based on more than four decades of professional experience, much of which has been concerned with the microfoundations of macromeasurement, especially in the productivity field. For example, in 1935-36, the author developed price index numbers for purchases of the Commonwealth Edison Company (wage rates, fuel, operating and maintenance materials, and capital equipment), using company records and drawing on the knowledge of staff accountants and engineers. In 1936-37, he participated in a pioneer effort to measure construction output and productivity from records of contractors and architects. In 1941-43, while assistant chief of a new productivity division in the U.S. Bureau of Labor Statistics, he directed studies of shipyards, aircraft assembly plants, petroleum refineries, as-yet unbuilt synthetic rubber facilities, and copper mines. In 1957-58, he served as technical consultant to the International Business Machines Corporation in the development of its productivity and unit-cost indexes for manufacturing. In 1973-79, while an economic advisor at the Department of Commerce, he lectured frequently to business and professional audiences on company productivity measurement and also participated in the design of performance-measurement systems for government.

Two additional sources of information for this book should be mentioned. One is an intensive review of the scattered relevant literature. The author has also benefited from observations and insights that many company officials and managers have shared with him over the years.

As the epigraph indicates, the primary intent of this monograph is the practical application of measurement arts. The author's specific objectives are to encourage and assist companies to track their own productivity changes—in the literal belief that such undertakings would be in the national interest as well as redound to private benefit.

Although the principal thrust of this book is practical, the result is not exactly a manual. For one thing, companies have different capabilities, structures, and needs, so they cannot realistically be offered a uniform set of prepackaged instructions. Furthermore, many issues of concept and method in productivity measurement in general remain unresolved. Some of these matters of "theory" are here addressed from the standpoint of company measurement and in the light of the author's own professional preferences. Algebraic elucidations are relegated to appendix notes—to avoid mathematical intimidation of the majority of the intended readers.

The author is grateful to Dr. E. Earl Wright, director of the W.E. Upjohn Institute for Employment Research, for encouragement in all stages of the preparation of this book. He also appreciates the assistance given by Judith K. Brawer and other members of the Institute staff in expeditiously transforming a manuscript into a publication.

Irving H. Siegel

Bethesda, MD
January 1980

Contents

Chapter 1
Orientation and Overview

The Subject

The theme of this monograph is fairly suggested by the title: Companies may help to raise their own productivity, significantly and relatively inexpensively, by measuring it. The direct effect of a company measurement program could be amplified by coordination with other extant or planned managerial undertakings to improve company performance. Furthermore, the extensive participation of companies in monitoring their own productivity could have a salutary spillover effect on the national base of "atomic" data, which is always inadequate to the varied demands of national policy.

The improvement of company productivity is ever a timely subject and nowadays seems even more so. Thus, against the backdrop of chronic inflation that plagued the late 1960s and the 1970s and still rages, it is clear that the survivability, autonomy, and profitability of companies are closely linked to ability to control costs of production. The upgrading of company performance, furthermore, ought to benefit the national productivity rate, which has slowed disappointingly in recent years. All Americans have a stake in the recovery of the national productivity pace—as a requisite for eventual mastery of inflation, for continuing competitiveness in world markets, and for the maintenance of high-level employment and customary living standards.

1

The Book and the Title

The content and structure of this book are succinctly summarized by key words in the remaining chapter titles. Thus, the next three chapters are concerned with the *why, what,* and *how* of company productivity measurement, and the final chapter offers some *examples.* Services as well as manufacturing, the traditional area of productivity measurement, are covered in the examples. Appendix notes expand a few of the remarks made in the text. The rest of this chapter touches selectively and briefly on topics treated later.

Two words in the title require early elucidation. First, "productivity" has many contemporary connotations, but it is restricted here to a preferred professional usage. It is defined, for the purposes of this monograph, as a family of ratios of quantity of output to quantity of input.[1] This "quantity form" is dimensionally equivalent to a "price form," which is also of practical and theoretical interest and will be considered at some length later.[2]

The second word requiring explication is "company." It here refers to company components also (e.g., divisions, plants, departments, and cost centers); and, less obviously, it is broadly construed to include government agencies and elements thereof (e.g., bureaus, offices, sections, and work centers).

Extension of the meaning of "company" to include government agencies is apt. Increased interest in the productivity of government operations at all levels has led to serious confrontation of the difficulties besetting the measurement of services in general. The progress made in measurement in the

---

1. By courtesy and convention, an output aggregate that is expressed in constant dollars (current dollars adjusted for price change) is regarded as a "quantity."

2. In index-number design, construction, analysis, and interpretation, it is important to distinguish between the mere satisfaction of a dimensional criterion and the satisfaction, in addition, of the stricter requirements of algebraic compatibility. An agreeable "cancellation of words" in a dimensional formula (verbal algebra) is not the same as the achievement of algebraic consistency in the detailed structures (aggregates) representing those words (literal algebra).

public sector is transferable to measurement relating to services performed in the private sector. It also has lessons for company measurement, whether in the services or in manufacturing.

Productivity Concepts

In the definition of "productivity" given above, the word "family" is not gratuitous. Although many different productivity measures are conceivable, the denominators most frequently encountered and most accessible to companies refer to labor input. Thus, a company that has decided to track its own productivity would be well advised to start, say, with global and detailed measures of output per employee-hour. (This ratio is dimensionally equivalent to the quotient of average hourly earnings of employees and unit labor cost—its price form.) Since capital (the other major "factor input" that is conventionally recognized) is difficult to quantify plausibly, a company would probably get an earlier positive payoff by proceeding next to measure output per unit of a significant "intermediate input," such as energy or a critical material. Most estimates of capital quantity are of doubtful quality, even if makers and users who want them badly are not inclined to show warranted circumspection. A "naive" alternative approach merits company consideration: the use of energy consumption as a proxy for capital services.

Recognition that productivity has a price form as well as the more conventional quantity form can aid in the design and interpretation of company measures. Many so-called "productivity" ratios, for example, do not satisfy our quantity definition, being "hybrids" with numerators expressed in current dollars (e.g., value added per man-hour).[3] From the price form, it is easy

---

3. Despite the preference for a strict productivity definition, this monograph recognizes, and explicitly states, that even crude measurement can help a company to improve its performance.

An appendix note (pp. 78-79) shows that a productivity change may be expressed approximately as a difference rather than a ratio. When the change is large, however, the approximation is poor. The same stricture applies to a fashionable use—or misuse—of mock calculus to define discrete productivity change as a difference between instantaneous rates of change in the numerator and the demonimator.

to see the algebraic linkage of such hybrids to the preferred quantity ratios (e.g., value added per man-hour is the product of output per man-hour and unit value added). Furthermore, for companies that have the necessary technical talent and data, an opportunity exists to construct productivity measures that meet the quantity and price criteria literally as well as dimensionally. Such sophisticated measurement systems would also routinely yield algebraically compatible cost indicators (e.g., unit value added). Since cost is a much more familiar accounting concept than productivity, a design that accommodates them both should appeal more strongly to skeptical executives.

End Products and Subproducts

The measurement of a company's or a government agency's output (and hence its productivity also) may focus either on end products or on subproducts. Typically, emphasis is placed on end products—on the final goods or services destined for markets or ultimate users. Every end product, however, may also be described, exhaustively and without double counting, as the sum of results (subproducts) emerging from a set of organizational subactivities.[4] A subactivity corresponds to a unitary process or coherent combination of such processes—to a work or cost center, to a sequence or cluster of such centers, or to a still larger component of organization (e.g., a company department or a government bureau).

A shift of emphasis in measurement from end products to subproducts could have many advantages. Subproducts are usually more homogeneous and, therefore, more amenable to arithmetic treatment. In short periods, they can also be matched more closely with their required inputs. They are suitable building blocks for output measures intended to meet general organizational needs (such as company planning and forecasting) and for

---

4. An end product may also be regarded as the immediate result of a terminal organizational subactivity. This fact correctly suggests that measurement in terms of end products without adjustment for inventory change could yield a distorted picture of a company's output performance.

consistent detailed measures intended to meet the needs of operational managers. Subproduct measurement also could point the way to rationalize production by, say, a reorganization of workflow or plant layout. Thus, it could help a company to avoid concentration on simply doing better what a company should no longer do at all.

A complete fine-grained monitoring system, however, also has drawbacks. It is less familiar than a system based on end products. More important is its expensiveness to implement and maintain. Apart from the cost of generating and recording adequate data is the cost of continual subproduct revision that the very success of the system may suggest. Accordingly, a company that undertakes monitoring may find it practical to start with a compromise between end product and subproduct measurement, as the next section proposes.

Company Systems and Strategies

Although many variables necessarily influence the actual shape of a monitoring program, a company is much more likely to embark on a two-tier program than to try construction of a comprehensive hierarchical battery of measures from the work (or cost) centers upward. Indeed, a company should begin on a modest scale rather than reach far beyond its grasp; and, if it does begin modestly, it can more comfortably change course along the way. After all, a measurement system is to some degree experimental; it should ideally remain evolutionary, adaptable to changing circumstances and requirements as these are revealed. The most important continuity is of the will—of top-level commitment and support.

A two-tier system attempts to accommodate simultaneously both the general needs of the helmsmen at headquarters and the specific needs of line management. Accepting the certainty that a comprehensive, integrated, "bottom-up" measurement system will be slow in developing and may never mature, it seeks broad company measures for use in such functions as forecasting, planning, and comparison against "the competition." At the same time, it moves toward monitoring subactivities on a selective basis. It focuses first on work centers, or on combinations having functional coherence, that are significant from the standpoint of cost, profitability, or continuity of production.

A company would do well to build on whatever foundations already exist, or at least to take them into account in a fresh approach. Where a "management information system" is in operation, for example, the periodic printouts may contain primitive productivity or quasi-productivity indicators that are not recognized as such. Where "work measurement" is practiced at all, a beachhead may be available for initiation of a more complete, formal system of subproduct monitoring through time. Even after a company has inaugurated, say, a dual-track program, it could benefit from review of its workflow and data base "as if" it were interested in the design of a hierarchical measurement system to accommodate the needs of headquarters and inward-looking management.

The time appears right for breaching the Chinese wall that too long has separated the "productivity measurement" art of the economic statistician and the "work measurement" art of the industrial engineer. The blending of these arts, to which some impetus should have been given by the recent and prospective advances in the assessment of government performance, would surely improve the outlook for integrated company measurement. Experience gained in a broader technical context might, for example, indicate the kinds of compromises that could reasonably be made in the combination of work centers and subactivities (to withstand the threats of reorganization to continuity of productivity time series) yet yield acceptable figures at manageable cost.

The statistician's approach has typically favored construction of output measures based on end products or final products, with acknowledgment made only indirectly of subproducts in the adjustment for inventory change. The engineer has typically concentrated on the measurement of a static "efficiency" ratio based on the "actual" and "standard" times required for the performance of an individual or small-group task. But, as an appendix note shows, such ratios may be "dynamized" and combined for many work centers to provide productivity measures of a kind preferred by the U.S. Bureau of Labor Statistics. A convergence, in short, is perceivable as the statistician's art develops downward toward work centers and as the engineer's extends upward—to a meeting at the subproduct interface.

Whatever choice a company makes, the specific design and installation of a monitoring system will surely not be trauma-free. The task force or steering group chartered by high company authority must gain the confidence of managers of other esteemed cost-control systems already in the field. It needs to enlist lower-echelon employees in the selection of measurement criteria and in other ways to make them feel that the system is "theirs." It has to review existing data bases, start two-tier measurement, "sell" the system with seminars and briefings, write instructions, designate "local" productivity officers, arrange for training, engage outside consultants, and provide a blueprint for future evolution and conduct of the measurement program. Guided by a vision of the ultimate or ideal system, it should nevertheless proceed by realistic incremental steps toward phased subgoals. It should keep responsibility for delivery of a "turnkey" operation, using outsiders for assistance only on specific technical tasks. Obviously, the list of cautions could be lengthened formidably; but comfort should also be taken from the experience that even a crude initial measurement effort can help raise productivity and that serious analysis and interpretation may compensate in some degree for limitations of the emerging figures.

Chapter 2
Why Companies Do or Should
Measure Their Productivity

The Setting

American businessmen have been obliged by economic changes since the mid-1960s to become more explicitly concerned with company productivity improvement. By their actions, if not in their verbal styles, they have traditionally shown an appreciation of the relevance of productivity growth to the survivability, autonomy, and profitability of their companies. But new circumstances making such growth uncertain have also transformed "productivity" into a buzzword and byword of the corporate annual report, the business magazine, the congressional committee print, and the one-day seminar announcement.[1]

---

1. The "new prominence of productivity," a leading businessman has noted, is only a "semantic development." In the 1920s, the fashion was to talk instead of "control of costs, efficiency, meeting competition, etc." (M.P. Venema, in *Defense Management Journal,* October 1972, p. 7.) In "A Half Century of American Productivity Measurement," an invited review paper presented by the present author at the 1950 meeting of the American Statistical Association, it was observed that "productivity still plays its most vital role under assumed names," in contrast to the practice of planned societies, "where governments have the responsibility for raising productivity and . . . use every available organ to this end."

Although the slowdown recorded in the national productivity advance in recent years is not fully understood,[2] a few adverse circumstances are widely believed to be contributory:

• The persistence of unprecedented rates of inflation, which (a) impedes acquisition of capital for replacement, expansion, pollution control, and worker safety; (b) limits private funds devoted to research, development, and innovation; and (c) threatens customary living scales.

• The revolution in world prices of petroleum and in conditions of supply.

• The proliferation of government-sponsored "regulation" and "paperwork."

• The apparent deterioration of employee attitudes, expressed in increasing "alienation" and erosion of the "work ethic."

The current setting favors discovery and adoption by many more companies of productivity monitoring as a low-cost means of spurring productivity gain. Evidence of company interest in this tool goes back to World War I or earlier—if we include the narrow preoccupation of Taylorism and "scientific management" with individual or group performance in circumscribed repetitive tasks.[3] But now, as then, only a very tiny fraction of the firms that

---

2. In the author's judgment, too little attention has been directed in the media, and even in professional discussions, to technical problems of measurement that can no longer be neglected with impunity in a prolonged, serious inflation. An influential professional discussion is contained in the last chapter of E.F. Denison, *Accounting for Slower Economic Growth: The United States in the 1970s,* The Brookings Institution, Washington, 1979, pp. 122-47. Another discussion, by J.R. Norsworthy and M.J. Harper, focuses on *The Role of Capital Formation in the Recent Productivity Slowdown* (Working Paper 87, Office of Productivity and Technology, U.S. Bureau of Labor Statistics, January 1979).

3. That many companies were in a position to compile figures on their own productivity by the beginning of the century is suggested by the work of C.D. Wright, the first U.S. Commissioner of Labor [Statistics]—e.g., his *Sixth Annual Report* (1891), a 1,400-page study of the iron and steel industry, and his celebrated *Thirteenth Annual Report* (1898), a 2,000-page study of "hand and machine labor." It is also known that "work measurement" was practiced early in the century in the Boston and Mare Island shipyards and in the Rock Island arsenal; and that time-study techniques attracted sufficient opposition to force their ban in such facilities in 1911 and in federal agencies in 1914-15.

might find measurement a sound minor investment appear to have formal systems in place. Even in manufacturing, where measurement is reputed to be easiest, this seems to be the case.[4]

In addition to the new circumstances forcing attention to self-monitoring is the increasing federal commitment to performance measurement for managerial purposes—a phenomenon bound to encourage some imitation in the private services and

---

Some impetus must have been given to company self-monitoring as the Bureau of Labor Statistics collected information for interplant comparisons in several industries in the 1920s and 1930s and began publishing industry productivity indexes in 1926. The Bureau's interestablishment comparisons for a few defense industries during World War II could also have had a benign demonstration effect; but much more influential on company practice was its program of securing "direct" reports on unit labor requirements from plants in a number of industries, a program begun in 1946 and discontinued in the early 1950s as too expensive. Studies conducted by the National Research Project of the Works Progress Administration in the late 1930s provided another opportunity for companies to learn to monitor their own productivity performance.

4. On the apparently limited current practice of monitoring in manufacturing, see I.H. Siegel, "Measurement of Company Productivity," in *Improving Productivity Through Industry and Company Measurement,* National Center for Productivity and Quality of Working Life, Washington, October 1976, pp. 15-16. In 1972, an assumption initially made in administration of the Economic Stabilization Program—that companies could "calculate their current and anticipated productivity trends and simply provide the appropriate documentation"—proved false, and government estimates for 400 industries had to be used as second-best instead. (See J.J. Carr, "Measuring Productivity," *The Arthur Andersen Chronicle,* March 1973, especially pp. 10-11; "How to Compute Productivity Gains," Publication 5-3020 (Rev. 6-72), Economic Stabilization Program; and J.W. Kendrick, "The Productivity Factor in Phase 2," *The Conference Board Record,* March 1972, pp. 28-35.)

Shortly after World War II, a National Industrial Conference Board questionnaire revealed that, "although . . . there is an interest in labor productivity, few plants have quantitative information on this subject." (Reported by Martin Gainsbrugh in *Summary of Proceedings of Conference on Productivity,* October 28-29, 1946, Bulletin No. 913, U.S. Bureau of Labor Statistics, Washington, p. 12.) The BLS program of direct reporting mentioned in footnote 3 certainly increased the visibility of companies engaging in productivity measurement. (See G.E. Sadler and Walter Hirsch, *Use of Productivity Data in American Manufacturing Establishments,* processed, U.S. Bureau of Labor Statistics, Washington, July 1949.) Contemporary articles also disclosed that some firms had measurement systems. (See, for example, Geoffrey Heyworth, "Productivity," *Advanced Management,* March 1951, pp. 14-18, which related to work measurement at Lever Brothers and Unilever; and William Langenberg, "An Experiment in Productivity Measurement," *N.A.C.A. Bulletin,* January 1952, Section 1, pp. 584-95, which related to measurement of output per unit of labor and nonlabor input at Johnson & Johnson.)

service industries.[5] As more company executives come to recognize the desirability of measurement, they will find sizable professions ready to assist in the design and implementation of monitoring programs—not only statisticians, engineers, econometricians, accountants, and managers, but also operations researchers, systems analysts, numerical analysts, managerial economists, and management scientists. The ubiquity of electronic computers and terminals and of programmers and other persons trained to operate them will also help to make company productivity-tracking a "cost-effective" proposition.

"Everything Has Two Handles"

The rewards promised for company productivity monitoring are attractive; but every management initiative, this one included, involves risk and requires care. A tool cannot, by mere existence, achieve the objective to which it is only instrumental; nor can it, by mere existence, atone for prior errors and neglects. It has to be introduced with discreet regard for the climate of labor-management relations and for the mix of control programs already deployed or pending. Furthermore, once a tool becomes available, it should be used, and used credibly and fairly; for a tool unused will rust or degrade to a toy, and a tool misused can become a dangerous or destructive weapon.

---

5. Circular No. A-117, sent by the Office of Management and Budget to the heads of all executive agencies on March 23, 1979, offered guidance on "management improvement" and "evaluation." It stated the policy that "all agencies . . . will assess the effectiveness of their programs and the efficiency with which they are conducted and seek improvement on a continuing basis." It defined "management improvement" as "any action taken to improve the quality and timeliness of program performance, increase productivity, control costs, or mitigate adverse aspects of agency operations." It defined "management evaluation" as "formal assessment of the efficiency of agency operations"—of "the effectiveness of organizational structures and relationships, operating procedures and systems, and work force requirements and utilization." It specifically requested "continuing attention . . . to management improvement and cost reduction opportunities in activities such as accounting, ADP operations, cash management, communications, data collection, grants management, paperwork, printing and reproduction, regulations improvement, travel, and other administrative activities." (See article by Yamada, cited in footnote 14, on Circular No. A-44, 1972 revision, which A-117 rescinds and supersedes.)

Reliance upon numbers in the regulation of human affairs poses special problems that cannot be ignored with impunity. Numbers are obviously inadequate for capturing all the relevant nuances of output and input, and they sometimes seem to miss altogether the essence of a productive activity. But nonquantitative methods have their own egregious limitations and idiosyncrasies and are notoriously subject to abuse. The trick, then, is to employ numerical procedures advantageously and well where they are especially appropriate—as they are in monitoring. A short, shrewd injunction by the philosopher Whitehead comes to mind: "Seek simplicity—distrust it." Numbers simplify by omission; analysis and interpretation express distrust and rectify omission.

A decision to monitor does not imply the acceptance of any standard system. A company should act according to its understanding of its needs and its technical and financial capabilities. The program that is adopted should not be too ambitious in scope, scale, and time schedule. A company that wants an articulated system to cover its total activity and spotlight the workings of its principal parts (e.g., divisions) may apply the subproduct concept lightly. On the other hand, a company that has an elaborate system of work measurement could easily adapt it to the requirements of a monitoring program for higher-echelon use. Measurements that are deemed suitable for a bonus scheme may be very far from satisfactory for the rating of jobs and the payment of wages. Where rapport between labor and management is good, where analysis and interpretation are already accepted as necessary complements of measurement, and where it is already agreed that the monitoring system is evolutionary, even crude numbers can be constructively and harmoniously used.[6]

---

6. As will be noted later in this book, companies operating under the Scanlon Plan are able to make bonus payments amicably in accordance with "productivity" formulas that do not satisfy our productivity definition. In answer to a question raised by the Joint Economic Committee, the Deputy Director of the Council on Wage and Price Stability observed that the performance criterion used under these plans "is most often measured in dollars rather than units of output," so "an increase in price is often called a 'productivity increase.'" (*The 1979 Economic Report of the President,* Hearings before the Joint Economic Committee, Washington, 1979, Part 3, p. 99.)

Implicit in the preceding paragraphs is the criticality of management. The best management (at all levels) shows its caliber by ability to manage itself. In addition to making the right choices and decisions, it is prepared to do what could not be anticipated when plans were made and roles were assigned. It assures project completion and deals with people not as "human resources" but as "resourceful humans."

Reported Company Uses of Monitoring Data

Representatives of companies that monitor productivity have on occasion commented publicly or disclosed to government officials the benefits accruing from the process of measurement or from application of the generated data. A few of the accessible appraisals are cited below—before the author presents an account of company benefits distilled from his own experience and from information imparted by cognizant company executives, managers, and technicians.

In 1949, when a war-devastated Europe and Japan eagerly sought the secrets of the U.S. productivity miracle, the Bureau of Labor Statistics (BLS) made a study for the Anglo-American Productivity Council on ways in which companies were using their own data in conjunction with published statistics. Among the published statistics were those developed by the Bureau for various manufacturing industries from direct company reports on man-hours required per unit of output of major products. The productivity figures were found to be used for education of junior executives and managers, for comparison of company performance against that of an industry as a whole, for review and modification of cost-accounting systems, for evaluation of extant work-measurement and job-rating programs, for checking on plant layout and work methods, for initiation or administration of bonus and incentive awards, for estimating practical capacity and future production, for cost control, for location of new plants, and for choice of new equipment and manufacturing procedures.[7]

7. G.E. Sadler and Walter Hirsch, *op. cit.* Among the industries covered in the BLS direct reporting program were: cane sugar, men's shirts, footwear, luggage, leather, fertilizers, soap, machinery, mining equipment, electrical appliances, and radio receivers.

In 1950, a technical mission of the Organization for European Economic Cooperation came to study measurement methods of BLS. It commented on the utility of company and industry statistics for gauging performance compared to competitors; for pinpointing departments needing improvement; for ascertaining what organizational structures, processes, and wages systems were superior from the standpoint of productivity; for planning changes in plant size and in the distribution of production among plants; and for revision of cost-accounting and other control systems.[8]

An internal report of the International Business Machines Corporation, prepared in 1958, commented on the uses of the new indexes of manufacturing and unit cost constructed with the author's technical assistance. The measures were seen as tools for management—for better appraisal of performance, for diagnosis of defective operations, and for indicating corrective action to be taken in such instances. They were also regarded as helpful in planning, particularly to avoid overbuilding and overhiring. An expected by-product was closer integration with, and improvement of, cost accounting.[9]

An examination of productivity-improvement systems of five companies, made by the National Center for Productivity and Quality of Working Life in 1975, confirmed that subproduct and more conventional work measurement could play important roles. "A measuring system," according to the canvassed companies, "brings some improvement in performance by making people more aware of the meaning of productivity." Measurement for organizational units is especially effective if used for setting goals and checking on accomplishment—e.g., goals for scrap reduction, energy saving, or output increase. In general, companies were said to adopt, or more diligently to pursue, programs of productivity improvement with such objectives as: strengthening competitive-

8. *Measurement of Productivity,* Organization for European Economic Cooperation, Paris, October 1952, p. 40.

9. S.H. Wareham, *Developing Indexes of Productivity and Unit Costs,* processed, International Business Machines Corporation, March 1958, p. 12.

ness in domestic or foreign markets, acquiring greater flexibility in response to external conditions, cost control and conservation acquisition of funds for capital investment, and payment of fair wages.[10]

It is also pertinent to mention the benefits claimed for productivity monitoring in government. As already noted, the position taken in this monograph is that company measurement, especially in the services, has much to gain from experience in public agencies. An authoritative summary of the uses of productivity measurement in operational and budgetary management was provided in 1977 by the Joint Financial Management Improvement Program, a cooperative undertaking of the Office of Management and Budget, the General Accounting Office, the Treasury Department, and the Civil Service Commission chartered by the Congress in 1950. Nine areas of potential application were specifically cited: goal-setting, estimation of resource requirements, budget justification, cost reduction, organizational improvement, control of operations, resource reallocation, manager accountability, and motivation of managers and other employees.[11]

Thirty years earlier, in 1947, while the author was Chief Economist of the Veterans Administration, a subproduct approach was taken for central-office monitoring of performance and control of staffing in numerous geographically dispersed field stations. When this agency was reorganized in 1953, the theme was to decentralize authority to the field offices; standard position descriptions and tables of organization were scrapped. Accordingly, it was necessary to develop and install comprehensive and detailed work-measurement systems for effective and continuous monitoring. These systems were intended to aid first-line supervisors in overseeing day-to-day operations, to enforce the concept of hierarchical managerial responsibility, and to facilitate

---

10. *Improving Productivity: A Description of Selected Company Programs,* National Center for Productivity and Quality of Working Life, Washington, December 1975, pp. 1-2.

11. *Implementing a Productivity Program: Points to Consider,* Joint Financial Management Improvement Program, Washington, March 1977, pp. 20-27.

interstation comparisons of performance. Thus, measurement and management were completely integrated in the interest of providing to veterans high-quality services at tolerable cost.[12]

Especially since the 1960s, the Department of Defense has also engaged in comprehensive, detailed, and hierarchical work measurement to facilitate (1) day-to-day matching of workloads and staff and (2) higher-echelon control, allocation, and planning with respect to manpower and funds. A leader in this movement was the Defense Supply Agency, which, like the Veterans Administration, needed to balance "decentralized operational responsibility and authority" with "centralized policy direction and performance appraisal" in carrying out its mission.[13]

Despite such examples, a company should recognize that the short logical step from the compilation of fine-grain productivity data to their actual incorporation in the budget process turns out to be a long and difficult step in practice. This fact is highly relevant to a company's level of commitment to monitoring and to its warranted expectations. Significantly, the General Accounting Office was still able to report in 1978 only spotty use of productivity information in federal budgeting (a directive of the Office of Management and Budget of 1972 notwithstanding). This finding was noted in a 1979 staff study of the Joint Economic Committee, which failed, however, to appreciate that the remedy could not lie in the expansion of a Bureau of Labor Statistics program of measuring federal productivity change in "major functional areas." The BLS indexes refer to the end products of agency bureaus or divisions, while serious budgetary applications would require hierarchical measurement down to (or, rather, up from) the work center. In 1977, after the concept of "zero-based

---

12. A good statement on the measurement program adopted for the era of decentralized authority is provided in *Development and Use of the Work Measurement and Performance Standards System,* Department of Veterans Benefits, Veterans Administration, Washington, December 1958.

13. P.G. Poulos, "Challenging DOD Management to Improve Internal Productivity," *Defense Management Journal,* April 1977, pp. 34-40; M.H. Baker, "Productivity Management in the Defense Supply Agency," *Public Administration Review,* November-December 1972, pp. 771-76.

budgeting" came on the federal scene, the author participated in a task force study that proposed a second track of government productivity measurement geared to managerial needs at all levels, including budget-making and review. The study contemplated continuation of the BLS system for present uses, such as interagency comparison of performance in the same functional areas.[14]

Rounded Summary of Benefits[15]

All the potential contributions of productivity measurement to the upgrading of productivity performance may be subsumed under three heads:

1. Assistance in efficient conduct of operations.
2. Improvement of internal company climate.
3. Assistance in coping with the external environment.

---

14. G.T. Yamada, "Improving Management Effectiveness in the Federal Government," *Public Administration Review,* November-December 1972, pp. 764-770; *Productivity in the Federal Government,* Joint Economic Committee, U.S. Congress, May 31, 1979, pp. 2, 8, 10-11; Charles Ardolini and Jeffrey Hohenstein, "Measuring Productivity in the Federal Government," *Monthly Labor Review,* November 1974, pp. 13-20; and W.E. Beasley, D.H. Dobelbower, and I.H. Seigel, *Toward Strengthening the Federal Productivity Program: A Report to the Federal Personnel Management Project from the Federal Productivity Work Group,* Assistant Secrtary for Administration, U.S. Department of Commerce, Washington, 1977.

15. Based largely on lectures given by the author to business and professional audiences (with opportunity for question-and-answer feedback) under the auspices of the U.S. Department of Commerce in 1975-79. (A summary of the author's remarks made at a Dayton seminar in February 1975 appears in *Productivity Enhancement in Logistical Systems,* U.S. Department of Commerce, Washington, May 1975, pp. 27-32, 144-47; at a Pittsburg meeting in June 1975, in the Department's *Situation Report,* Productivity Series, Bulletin 6, August 1975; and at a Los Angeles conference in December 1978, in a periodical of the Manufacturing Productivity Center of Illinois Institute of Technology, *Manufacturing Productivity Frontiers,* March 1979, pp. 1-4).

A new report, *Measurement and Interpretation of Productivity* (National Academy of Sciences, Washington, 1979), contains a chapter on company measurement that is consistent, on the whole, with the summary presented here. The chapter acknowledges that "a company can improve its performance by developing its own measurement system" (p. 166), but then offers only a flaccid recommendation: that "companies investigate whether having measures of productivity would improve their performance, planning, and evaluation" (p. 174). The same recommendation "encourages the U.S. Department of labor and the U.S. Department of Commerce to continue to inform companies of the potential benefits of productivity measurement programs" (p. 174).

From the standpoint of the company's productive activity (operations), these three categories may be characterized as looking *at,* looking *around,* and looking *out.* A brief, rounded statement of the benefits obtainable from a company program of productivity monitoring is presented in this triple sequence in the paragraphs that follow.

The first category of benefits relates particularly to a measurement system that is already functioning. As the numbers become available, they may be examined, analyzed, interpreted, and discussed; and, subjected to such review, they are likely to offer some ground for action. A minimum indicated action may be improvement of the measurement system itself—e.g., by elimination of remaining "bugs" or "noise," by change in output or input units of reckoning, or by extension of the scope, scale, or detail of monitoring. But the numbers could also provide timely clues to the emergence or existence of operational imbalances or dysfunctions that require adjustment. Furthermore, after corrective action is taken, the numbers permit before-and-after comparisons for appraisal of the efficacy of the "fix."

Additional potential uses of the numbers in guiding operations merit notice. Numbers could, for example, assist efforts at overhead "control by ratio"—at making or keeping the proportion of "indirect" labor "as small as possible although as large as necessary" to support a level of company output. They may also suggest plausible targets and time tables for future accomplishments in production and productivity. They provide a "bottom line" for assessing the net impact of company programs that ought to enhance productivity (e.g., work simplification, job enrichment, incentive awards, management by objectives, resource conservation, and quality control). The more detailed and the more numerous the series included in the measurement battery, the more sensitive and more versatile will the monitoring system be. But, as already noted, a company has to balance its felt needs against its technical and financial competency.

The second category of benefits may begin to be experienced even *before* numbers become available. Thus, the "announcement effect" could be electric, heightening awareness at all staff levels of the importance of getting more output from a given input or of reducing the input required for a given output. Of course, the more congenial the original climate of labor-management relations, the better will be the response to announcement of a productivity-monitoring venture.

A measurement program that contemplates the monitoring of one or more subactivities in addition to a more general surveillance of company performance offers an opportunity for also experiencing an "enlistment effect." The help of employees could be solicited in the selection of eligible areas for special scrutiny and in the selection of measurement criteria. Such participation assures fuller cooperation in the program.

Substantial contributions to rapport may also be expected from analysis, interpretation, and discussion of the numbers. The review process provides occasion for intercommunication of all levels of management and of lower-level management with the operating staff. Valuable suggestions could emerge with respect to organization of the work, plant layout, hearing of grievances, etc. The numbers, in short, provide agenda for a progressive dialogue between management and labor—a dialogue confined at first to explicit productivity issues and then, as trust grows, expanding to cover additional topics of mutual concern.

When a company has multiple facilities performing common operations or supplying similar services in different parts of the country, comparison can prove tonic to the productivity of the company as a whole. Why is one facility consistently superior to another? Why does a facility falter in one period or change in ranking? Answers to such questions have to be based on analysis, and the asking and responding are vital to management accountability and to elimination of slack.

The third category of benefits is concerned with forecasting, planning, and interfirm competition. The projection of productivity figures and their use in conjunction with others for the company, its industry, and the economy can help shape decisions and strategies important for survival, autonomy, and profitability. Comparison of a company's productivity trend against that of its industry can lead to searching questions, trenchant analysis, and constructive action. For such comparison, a company may find valuable the labor productivity series published for various industries by the Bureau of Labor Statistics and by some trade associations. The Department of Energy has issued industry measures of energy productivity that should also prove useful. Quasi-productivity operating ratios compiled for some 600 manufacturing industries and industry groups by the Census Bureau could likewise provide guidance for the coping of companies with their external environments.[16]

---

16. See, for example, *Productivity Indexes for Selected Industries,* Bulletin 2002, U.S. Bureau of Labor Statistics, Washington, 1978; *Voluntary Business Energy Conservation Program Progress Report* No. 6, U.S. Department of Energy, Washington, April 1978; and *Annual Survey of Manufactures, 1976: Industry Profiles,* U.S. Bureau of the Census, May 1978.

Chapter 3
What Productivity Is and Is Not

Definition

To define "productivity" as a serious term of art or "science" might seem like searching for safe passage between Charybdis and Scylla, which Odysseus found only with the help of Athena. Successful definition requires that we steer clear of the whirlpools of confused popular usage and at the same time avoid being sucked into caverns of esoteric connotation. Strangely, if we go back to the professional literature of the 1940s, 1950s, and 1960s, before "productivity" became a buzzword and byword of daily parlance, the task of definition becomes less formidable. In those decades (and earlier), students of the subject had to justify to academic brethren an interest in time series showing changes in *average* productivity rather than in static *production functions* more concerned with *marginal* productivity. But they already had in clear view a notion very much like the one we adopt for this monograph:

Productivity is a family of ratios of (a) quantity of output to (b) quantity of related resource input.

"Quantity of" could be replaced by "real," a common synonym in the economic vocabulary, without alteration of sense.[1]

This definition keeps the term free of unquantifiable irrelevancies yet accommodates a considerable diversity of professional emphasis. It is deceptively simple yet states adequately what economic statisticians and econometricians generally mean to do when they undertake to measure productivity. The nouns and adjectives require further discussion, however, and it is to this task that most of the remainder of this chapter is devoted. We say "most" because attention is also directed toward meanings *not* in accord with the strict professional signification that we prefer. Too many discussions involving productivity degenerate into mad tea parties because well-intentioned Alices think that saying what one means and meaning what one says are "the same thing, you know."

Although it is not essential at this point, it is not gratuitous either to note that the above definition of "productivity" is equivalent to another. The alternative formulation is more rarely encountered in the literature, but it is also germane to measurement, analysis, and theory and has a special relevance (usually unnoticed) to governmental programs of wage and price restraint—as may be seen from Appendix Note 1. Thus, instead of speaking of ratios of output and input quantities, we may define "productivity" as *a family of ratios of (a) input price to (b) output price.*

The equivalence of the two definitions is evident from dimensional algebra—or, as it might also be called, "verbal" algebra. More important for measurement, however, is the

---

1. In 1946, Solomon Fabricant, who has long been the dean of American productivity measurement, used "productivity" in the sense here preferred. (See *Summary of Proceedings of Conference on Productivity,* Bulletin No. 913, U.S. Bureau of Labor Statistics, pp. 2-3.) Essentially the same definition was used later by H.S. Davis in *Productivity Accounting,* University of Pennsylvania Press, Philadelphia, 1955, pp. 2-3, and J.W. Kendrick in *Productivity Trends in the United States,* Princeton University Press, Princeton, 1961, pp. 6-7. In "A Half Century of American Productivity Measurement," an invited paper presented at the 1950 meeting of the American Statistical Association, the present author also embraced what then seemed to be the standard definition, noting the multiplicity of relevant ratios and their expression in "real" terms.

realizability of this equivalence in "literal" algebra, as Appendix Note 1 also demonstrates. Literal algebra—the kind taught in school—is concerned with the construction of appropriate aggregates and index numbers for macrovariables from detailed data for corresponding microvariables. More will be said later (in the discussion of the practice of deflation) about the common error of assuming that the "black boxes" of verbal identities and equations can be correctly filled without special attention to the basic micro-data and to the formulas for combining them.[2] It is pertinent to add here that the conventional quantity form of productivity will be given primacy in this monograph over the price form, but that the latter will not be relegated to the curio cabinet.[3]

Multiplicity of Admissible Productivity Ratios

From the definition, it is clear that, even as a term of art, "productivity" is an umbrella word covering a whole family of ratios. Not only is the family large but it also has many subfamilies. For example, when we speak of "output per man-hour," the most familiar of all productivity concepts, we may properly have many different varieties of output and man-hours in mind; and these varieties belong, in turn, to a still larger ensemble of measures of output per unit of labor input, a productivity subfamily.

---

2. For additional comment on the distinction between verbal and literal algebra, see, for example, I.H. Siegel, "On the Design of Consistent Output and Input Indexes for Productivity Measurement," in *Output, Input, and Productivity Measurement,* Princeton University Press, Princeton, 1961, pp. 23-41; and the last essay in his *Fuller Employment with Less Inflation,* W.E. Upjohn Institute for Employment Research, Kalamazoo, 1969, pp. 55-70.

3. Given the traditional preoccupation of the business community with costs and prices, the second definition might have more appeal than the first for company monitoring. This point will have to be left, however, to a future occasion—in deference to the judgment of Mme. de Staël, who criticized a book for having too many new ideas and not enough old ones.

No single variety or subfamily of productivity should, because of the ubiquity of basic data or the ease of computation, be regarded as the *true* representative of the whole family. The same caution applies to any *official* indicator of productivity. It also applies to any revelation that has dawned upon a member of the new "confessional school" of productivity experts after a "creative" inward search for "what productivity means to me."

The multiplicity of eligible measures of productivity derives from at least four sources. First, terms like "output" and "input" are themselves umbrella words, as already suggested. Second, index-number makers may appropriately exercise technical options as they do their jobs, choosing one set of units, weights, averages, or index formulas rather than another when they are not under contextual or other constraint. Third, limitations of the data supply may require substitutions, operational compromises, approximations, and indirect techniques that themselves increase the number of *de facto* variant measures. Finally, users seek and apply measures for a diversity of purposes and contexts, and this diversity on the demand side ideally requires the availability of many different indicators.

"Ratio" and "Quantity"

After "family," the next key words in the first of the two productivity definitions are "ratio" and "quantity." Both actually require more discussion than would at first appear necessary—especially because we have to deal with aggregates as well as single products and inputs, and with multiperiod and multiple-entity comparisons as well as measurements for single periods and firms.

Although output is the intended numerator of the productivity ratio and input is the intended denominator, it is often convenient to talk of reciprocals—of various inputs per unit of output. These inverse ratios are often innocuously described as "productivity" ratios, but they strictly represent "unit input requirements."

The quantity of a supposedly homogeneous output or input is often countable in more than one additive unit, in which case

(a) more than one productivity ratio is derivable and (b) these alternative ratios may show considerably different time traces. For example, the output of a particular automobile tire of constant quality through time may be reckoned by number, weight, or expected miles of service to users; a coal mine's production is measurable in tons or therms; a copper mine's output is expressible in tons of ore or of recoverable metal; an employment office could count referrals or placements. Since alternative output indicators may be expected to show different percentage changes through time, the same will be true of the variant productivity "relatives" (the quotients of productivity ratios for different periods with respect to the productivity ratio for a "base" or reference period).

When output includes two or more products or when input is composite, the distinguishable elements have to be weighted (for transformation to a common denominator) before aggregation. The weights most frequently used refer to prices of a particular period, in which case the aggregates are expressed in constant dollars of that period. Such dollars are, by courtesy and convention, regarded as measures of "quantity." They do, when correctly computed, represent money values in which the quantities remain unstabilized while prices have been fixed. Ratios of output or input aggregates that refer to different periods but incorporate the same set of weights are called "index numbers;" and the ratios of such output and input indexes are indexes of productivity. By a judicious selection of weights for the output and input measures, the derived productivity indicators may be endowed with attractive properties—as a concern for the difference between verbal and literal algebra makes clear and as our appendix notes demonstrate.

Although price weights are usually invoked (because of their general availability and "economic" overtones), other weights also are of interest. Among these alternatives are unit cost, unit labor cost, and unit labor requirements—for use in aggregating output. The weighting of products by unit labor requirements was probably innovated at the Works Progress Administration (WPA) National Research Project in the 1930s, and it was adopted by the

Bureau of Labor Statistics in the 1940s for the construction of various industry productivity indexes.[4] An index of output per man-hour computed as a ratio of (a) an output measure with weights referring to unit man-hour requirements and (b) an index of unweighted man-hours has attractive properties; it "condenses" to a single explicit ratio of weighted aggregates that is certain to be an internal average of the individual productivity relatives.[5] It is not widely appreciated that the same attractive properties would be possessed by the ratio of (a) a price-weighted output index and (b) an input measure in which the man-hours for each product are weighted in a special way. Appendix Note 2 discusses the WPA-BLS "condensing" productivity index and this less familiar alternative.

The weighting of output by unit man-hour requirements provides the key to a needed reconciliation of conventional productivity measurement, as practiced by the economic statistician, and conventional work measurement, as practiced by the industrial engineer. The two disciplines should be nudged toward a convergence, as Chapters 1 and 2 have suggested, at the subproduct or subactivity interface. Their junction, as blueprinted in Appendix Note 3 and the next paragraph, would be a boon to company productivity monitoring—to the use of measurement for management of operations and to the extension of measurement to service subactivities and service industries.

The condensed WPA-BLS productivity formula is an exact analogue of the engineer's ratio of standard hours to actual hours. Both refer to "should-take" hours and "did-take" hours, and

---

4. See *BLS Handbook of Methods for Surveys and Studies,* Bulletin 1910, U.S. Bureau of Labor Statistics, Washington, 1976, pp. 225-26; and Harry Magdoff, I.H. Siegel, and M.B. Davis, *Production, Employment, and Productivity in 59 Manufacturing Industries, 1919-36,* Philadelphia, National Research Project, Works Progress Administration, May 1939, Part 1, pp. 3-12.

5. An internal average of productivity relatives lies between the highest and lowest of them. This commonsense criterion unfortunately does not enjoy universal appeal, especially when an illusory or short-lived productivity bonus can be gained through a "shift effect" (e.g., on the national level, through the movement of agricultural workers into urban industry).

both implicitly treat man-hour sums as quantities. The WPA-BLS version is normally applied to the end products of establishments, while the engineer's normally applies to work centers or other narrow subactivities. The former is interpreted, as it ought to be, as a measure of change through time; the latter is typically interpreted as a static comparison of standard versus actual labor requirements ("efficiency") in a single period. For a try at comprehensive monitoring that would serve many needs of management (though too gross for budgeting, perhaps, or for setting pay scales), a company might wish to gerrymander its map of total activity into a reasonable number of well-defined subactivities characterized by significant measurable subproducts. In such an undertaking, the company should use "historical" standards as subproduct weights (i.e., actual unit man-hour requirements in the "base" or compared period) rather than "engineered" standards.

Five additional points merit mention before this section is brought to a close:

1. Whatever the unit chosen for counting the quantity of a product or an input, it is desirable to recognize the potentially confounding influence of quality change through time. Indeed, it may be preferable to avoid this influence in the first place or to correct for it[6]—e.g., by applying conversion factors that re-express a series in a new standard unit, by breaking a product or input into finer categories that are separately weighted, or by resort to such index-number techniques as "splicing" and "chaining." Of course, there is also a "cheap way out"—deflation, which is sought and tolerated in the absence of credible direct methods, is sanctioned by custom, and makes superficial sense according to verbal algebra even when it may be far from satisfying the standards of literal algebra.

2. In expositions of economic measurement, especially the construction and use of index numbers, it is natural to emphasize temporal change, but the methodology often applies

---

6. Input should obviously not be measured in "efficiency units" that show productivity to be constant through time.

equally to unitemporal comparisons—e.g., of facilities of the same company. Ideally, if two plants of the same company are compared in productivity performance over a wide range of products or subproducts, a valid interplant index should be constructed: The products should be fixed in kind and quality and they should be aggregated with the aid of the same set of weights. (Later, we shall refer to a case in which, unfortunately, weight standardization is impracticable—interestablishment comparisons of value added per man-hour.)

3. It is also preferable to use the same index-number criteria when comparing the time traces of productivity for (a) plants of the same company, (b) two firms in the same industry, or (c) a company and its industry. By fixing the scope and content, the weights, and the combining formula, we get a "purer" indication of the differences in productivity movements.

4. In the interpretation of (2) and (3) above, allowance should be made for the possibility that a purpose of comparison is to test the efficacy of alternative modes of organizing production. (Plants making similar end products may have different ways of sequencing or grouping subactivities or functions.)

5. The quantity of a company's output should preferably exclude rejects and returns; and reckoning in terms of subproducts should not mistake mere resource input for a valid step toward completion of a wanted good or service. It would be foolish for a company to strive to do more efficiently what should not be done at all—either in terms of end products or subproducts.

Output Concepts

To explicate the term "output" as used in the productivity definition, we note first that there are several categories of concepts. These differ in degree of correspondence to the span and structure of a company's productive activity, to the economic contribution assignable to the company's "factor" input. A company that intends to monitor its productivity should choose a numerator (and denominator) with due regard to the uses foreseen for the numbers—as well as to data availability, ease of computation, and other considerations of cost and convenience.

The first class of output concepts focuses on quantities of a company's end products of goods and services. Actually, such products are the subproducts of *final* subactivities, but they are intended to represent a company's entire effort. Nevertheless, they are *gross* in that they incorporate value not contributed by a company's factor input. In other words, *intermediate* inputs, such as purchased energy and materials, are also responsible for their existence.

Examples of the first class of output concepts are sales, shipments, deliveries, and completions. Quantities of such end products are typically weighted by price (or unit cost) for the purposes of aggregation. Sometimes, however, an attempt is made to "nettify" these quantities by the use of weights that more closely reflect the scope of a company's productive effort or its factor input; these weights refer, for example, to unit value added, unit labor cost, or unit labor requirements.

The second class of concepts may be alternatively regarded as just a variant of the first, but it embodies an important adjustment that makes it significantly different. Examples are sales and shipments adjusted for changes in inventories of finished goods and work in progress. These concepts attempt to convert a period's inventory flux into end-product equivalents. They are still gross, however, in the sense that they include the implicit contribution of purchased energy, materials, etc. The term "gross output" is commonly applied to such measures of production.

The third class of concepts is "net," including the venerable Census notion of "value added" and still netter variants suggested by the national income and product accounts kept by the Bureau of Economic Analysis of the U.S. Department of Commerce. These concepts start as money values, which can, however, be decomposed into the product of net-output quantity and gross price, or (as already hinted in the comment on the first class of output concepts) the product of gross-output quantity and net price. Census value added equals the value of gross output reduced by the cost of purchased energy, materials, etc. A netter value, analogous to the gross national product, also includes purchased business services (e.g., advertising and telephone) in the subtrahend. A still netter concept corresponds to the net national product or national income; the subtrahend here also includes indirect business taxes and an allowance for capital consumption.[7]

A net output index may be constructed in the same manner as a gross measure. Its weighted aggregates, however, are split, each containing a gross-output component that is diminished by an intermediate-input component. If price weights are used and if a factor-input measure can be constructed that corresponds exactly in scope to the value added defined by the net-output concept, a "condensed" productivity index is derivable. This productivity measure would not only be an internal average of the net productivity relatives but would also be an internal average of "partial" productivity indexes for the identified factors. The algebra of this case is shown in Appendix Note 4.

The fourth class of output concepts features "subproducts." As already indicated more than once in this monograph, these concepts deserve consideration by companies for control of operations and for monitoring of service activities. They may be used for defining exhaustively the same area that is covered by net output. The mapping may be as detailed as a company's data systems allow; it may concentrate on work centers, clusters or sequences thereof, decision units or decision packages, or functions, all of which contribute incrementally to the realization of end products.

The subproduct approach commends itself particularly where a company's end products are difficult to quantify without serious misgivings (e.g., because of extreme heterogeneity) or are too unreflective of the scope and structure of activity to yield a stable

---

7. Publications of the quinquennial Census of Manufactures contain a standard explanation of terms, including good concise descriptions of value added and some other concepts of interest to a company that intends to monitor its productivity. July issues of the *Survey of Current Business* contain sections on the national income and product accounts that would also be useful to such a company.

productivity measure. Thus, the approach may be especially welcome where a production cycle is long, where a dominant material is progressively shaped or processed into a "tree" of dissimilar end products, where make-or-buy policy is volatile, or where the scope of activity undergoes drastic change over time.[8]

Indexes of subproduct output may be constructed in the same manner as for gross output, with one important difference: An adjustment for inventory change becomes virtually unnecessary if a fine subproduct "mesh" is adopted. The weights may refer to unit total cost, unit value added, unit labor cost, or unit labor requirements—according to the verbal identity that the index-maker may wish to satisfy. The output of an overhead subactivity could either be treated as a separate subproduct or be represented by the subproducts that the subactivity logistically supports.

Where end products cannot satisfactorily be defined (as distinguished from *measured*), the subproduct approach may prove to no avail. The method actually takes its guidance from the list of specifiable end products, working *backward* to anatomize a company's total activity into functionally significant subactivities. Thus, a government agency charged with "defense" or "deterrence" has to translate such abstractions into an ensemble of final products within its capability (and sufficient for at least minimum discharge of its responsibility); then the breakdown of the agency's total activity into relevant subactivities becomes manageable. If "health" is first translated into something like "medical care," the latter may in turn be restated in terms of end products—and subproducts—of physicians' offices and hospitals. Banks, real estate sellers, and insurance companies that take the trouble of specifying the end results of their activities can, if they wish, go on to anatomization for more sensitive output and

---

8. For an early discussion of subproduct measurement that is still pertinent, see I.H. Siegel, "The Concept of Productive Activity," *Journal of the American Statistical Association,* June 1944, pp. 218-28. For a more recent discussion which talks of "cost centers" and "super cost centers" instead of subactivities and subproducts in monitoring the performance of "departments" or "functional areas," see J.J. Carr, "Measuring Productivity," *The Arthur Andersen Chronicle,* March 1973, pp. 8-19.

productivity measurement.[9] An activity such as research and development, which is speculative and has a long-deferred output (if any), does not seem amenable to quantitative treatment prospectively; but retrospective measurement of its output, once its end products become visible, is a different matter.[10]

Deflation

The indirect method of deflation—of division, usually, of an index of money value by a more or less relevant index of price—has great appeal as a way of deriving a measure of output (gross, net, or subproduct). It is far less arduous, as a rule, than the direct method of weighting individual quantities (or relatives) and adjusting the aggregates (or not) for omission of products not reported by quantity. The direct path, however, is often too forbidding, or impossible, to take for any distance—e.g., because of data gaps and discontinuities, extreme heterogeneity or quality change of products, and difficulty of (a) conceptualizing end products or (b) deriving a measure therefor that could satisfactorily depict productivity trend.

---

9. Useful discussion of measurement issues and strategies is to be found in V.R. Fuchs, ed., *Production and Productivity in the Service Industries,* Columbia University Press, New York, 1969, especially in the papers of M.W. Reder (on medical care) and David Schwartzman (on retail sales) and in comments by J.W. Kendrick (on life insurance) and N.E. Terleckyj (on life insurance and banking). Two more recent papers discuss output measures for life insurance "services" or "activities:" Ron Hirshhorn and Randall Geehan, "Measuring the Real Output of the Life insurance Industry," *Review of Economics and Statistics,* May 1977, pp. 211-19; and Randall Geehan, "Returns to Scale in the Life Insurance Industry," *Bell Journal of Economics,* Autumn 1977, pp. 497-514 (especially pp. 499-501).

Also relevant are two early reports concerned with government productivity measurement: *Measuring Productivity of Federal Government Organizations,* U.S. Bureau of the Budget, Washington, 1964; and *Measuring and Enhancing Productivity in the Federal Sector,* Joint Economic Committee, U.S. Congress, August 4, 1972. The latter is a staff study of the U.S. Civil Service Commission, General Accounting Office, and Office of Management and Budget based on data obtained from 17 participating agencies.

10. Two informed, but inconclusive, reports may be helpful to companies: J.T. Hall and R.A. Dixon, *Productivity Measurement in R&D,* NBS Technical Note 80, National Bureau of Standards, U.S. Department of Commerce, December 1975; and *R&D Productivity,* 2nd edition, Hughes Aircraft Company, Culver City, CA, 1978, the result of a continuing study directed by R.T. Ranftl.

Casually practiced, as it too frequently is, deflation may leave a mess of literal algebra behind a verbal screen. For example, the result may be mislabeled as an index of output expressed in constant prices of a particular year when the literal algebra could show that it is not. More serious is the common failure of the actual deflator to match the ideal one (which would *not* be technically required if it were obtainable) in content, structure, and weights. If the deflator refers to input price, the index it yields is closer to input than to output. Furthermore, if a proper ensemble of end products is not conceivable or definable, price also is not conceivable or definable. All this means that care should be exercised in the choice of deflator and that the user of the resulting output measure acquires a probably unexpected burden of interpretation.

Input Concepts

The last word in our first definition of productivity is "input," which, for the purpose of "interesting" measurement, has to be construed as something that *is* rather than in terms of what it *does*. No position is taken in this monograph on the causal connection between output and input—as expressible in a "production function," static or dynamic. Implicitly, however, this monograph does assume that productivity is *not* a disposable "residual" that could be eliminated if only we measured all inputs exhaustively or correctly. Indeed, our second definition of productivity suggests that efforts to explain productivity change away are otiose; a composite price index for output should *not* be expected to coincide with a composite price index for input, and, if the two are forced into equality for any interval by a particular mode of measurement, they would most likely diverge again thereafter.

The most familiar productivity denominators refer to labor input—to employment or man-hours. Such measures may be comprehensive, covering all classes of workers (including managers and, perhaps, proprietors), or they may be limited to certain important categories (e.g., so-called "production workers," direct labor, or office employees). Measures of man-hours sometimes distinguish between scheduled hours and actual hours at the workplace. A distinction could also be made between hours paid for and hours worked (excluding vacations, leave, and, perhaps, make-ready time and breaks).

Usually, numbers of employees or man-hours are added without the intervention of weights. This convention may be a carryover from demography or common daily experience; people are often added together without distinction as to age, sex, race, geographic location, income, education, or occupation. For productivity measurement, however, especially if coordinate appraisal of unit (labor or total) cost within the same index-number system is contemplated (see Appendix Note 1), it would be appropriate to distinguish man-hours according to rates of pay. Other differentiations could be made if they are required for perceived uses and if the necessary information is accessible.

The idea of measuring productivity with respect to both labor and capital, especially the two combined, is attractive, but a company would do well to confine attention at first to labor. The measurement of capital is fraught with special difficulties for which the measurement of labor does not at all prepare. Caveats concerning deflation and literal versus verbal algebra typically have to be ignored. The resulting numbers often appear acceptable, not according to their intrinsic sense but in the light of the effort required and the need that is felt. Before extending the monitoring system to include capital, a company measurement team should make a thoughtful literature review and note particularly that scholars still argue, even heatedly, about concepts and methods.[11]

---

11. See especially the spirited exchange between D.W. Jorgenson and Zvi Griliches on the one side and E.F. Denison on the other in *Survey of Current Business,* May 1972, Part II. Also pertinent, but even headier, is G.C. Harcourt, *Some Cambridge Controversies in the Theory of Capital,* Cambridge University Press, London, 1972.

A recent action by the Financial Accounting Standards Board may in time make it easier for companies to track their real capital input. For fiscal years ending after Christmas 1979, enterprises are required to report supplementary information (e.g., on assets and depreciation) in terms of current cost as well as conventional historical cost. See *Statement of Financial Accounting Standards No. 33: Financial Reporting and Changing Prices,* Financial Accounting Standards Board, Stanford, September 1979.

Limitation of productivity monitoring in the first instance to labor really does not handicap a company as much as might be supposed. Labor is still a generally significant element of production cost, and it participates in virtually every company subactivity. Even without prior weighting, a labor total appears intelligible. After decades of repetition, it ought to be clear that confinement of the productivity denominator to man-hours does not at all imply that no other factor contributes to output; even the "labor theory of value" of the 19th century did not entertain so naive a view. Finally, and most important, a company can compensate somewhat, by analysis and interpretation of the numbers, for omission of other factors in measurement.

An attempt to measure capital in physical terms is, willy nilly, a metaphysical exercise also. As in the case of other produced commodities, equipment quantities have to be adjusted to abstract in some sense from quality change (but not explicitly for change in productivity potential). All acquisition prices have to be translated to a common base period—but the same item might not have been produced or producible in that period. Often it is necessary to disentangle quantities from book values that are aggregates for items of different model, size, vintage, age, price, and technology; and the money values may be heavily compromised by tax and accounting considerations and conventions.

Another kind of challenge is presented by the fact that a capital stock has three faces: (1) it comprises heterogeneous end products made in prior years, (2) it is available for current production of other goods and services, and, (3) according to its capacity and remaining lifetime, it is a projection of the goods and services derivable from its future use. Reconciliation of these three aspects in one indicator may not be possible. One attempt suggests a role for projected output in the measurement of current capital input with suitably adapted base-period prices as weights. Such a measure would be compatible with a wage-weighted labor indicator for measurement of composite productivity.[12]

12. I.H. Siegel, "Design of Consistent Indexes for Capital Quantities and Associated Variables," *Bulletin of the International Statistical Institute,* Vol. 43 (1969), Book 1, pp. 275-90; and "Capital Index-Number Design," *1970 Proceedings of the Business and Economic Statistics Section, American Statistical Association,* pp. 619-20.

According to the usual view of capital measurement, a company that wants to include this second factor in its monitoring program has several practical options. It may be satisfied with a series representing total fixed investment or capital stock (land, buildings, and equipment), gross of depreciation and revalued in constant prices of a base period. It may instead prefer a net version, which reflects deductions for depreciation. If it is more ambitious, it could go on to include working capital or all the assets shown on the balance sheet. Thus, using such deflators as seem appropriate and are at hand, it could restate cash, accounts receivable, material inventories, goods inventories, etc., in constant prices of the same base period and obtain comprehensive estimates of real capital.

The aggregates for real capital could be combined with labor input for measuring composite productivity. The base-period rate of return, or unit rental value, could serve as the weight for capital, and labor input would have the same dollar dimension. (Incidentally, the discussion to this point has ignored leased capital, which ought also to be included, with a suitable weight, in the denominator for measuring composite productivity.)[13]

Whether or not a company proceeds to cover capital in addition to labor in its monitoring system, it may wish to track its performance with respect to intermediate inputs. Thus, in the current economic setting, an interest would be natural in the time trace of output per unit of fuel or energy input, or output per unit of a critical high-grade material. Reduction of a company's reject rate conserves energy and material as well as labor. A company

---

13. For fuller treatment of capital measurement at the company level, see H.S. Davis, *op. cit.*; J.W. Kendrick and Daniel Creamer, *Measuring Company Productivity: Handbook with Case Studies,* The Conference Board, New York, 1965; and Leon Greenberg, *A Practical Guide to Productivity Measurement,* Bureau of National Affairs, Washington, 1973. Also of potential value to a company that has decided to go beyond labor input are: D.L. Cocks, "The Measurement of Total Factor Productivity for a Large U.S. Manufacturing Corporation," *Business Economics,* September 1974, pp. 7-20; and C.E. Craig and R.C. Harris, "Total Productivity Measurement at the Firm Level," *Sloan Management Review,* Spring 1973, pp. 13-29. Less satisfactory, but still of possible interest, is B.W. Taylor III and K.R. Davis, "Corporate Productivity—Getting It All Together," *Industrial Engineering,* March 1977, pp. 32-36.

that is satisfied with its measure of capital may feel encouraged to go the rest of the way and estimate productivity for all its intermediate inputs and for factor and intermediate inputs combined.[14]

In closing this section, we call attention to the possibility of using energy consumption (for heating and lighting of plant and for operation of equipment) as a plausible surrogate for capital services. Where such use appears valid, the tortuous estimation of real capital stock for the purpose of productivity measurement could be circumvented. After all, when real capital stock is weighted by a constant rate of return, the result, in effect, is a measure of capital services. The stratagem of enlisting energy consumption as a double-duty measure should prove attractive as an economical shortcut or as a provisional expedient.

What Productivity Is Not

Having concluded discussion of productivity as a family of ratios of output quantity to input quantity, we turn to a consideration of other, less satisfactory or even incorrect, meanings. Strangely, despite professional usage of many decades, our definition has no foothold in the dictionary.[15] Furthermore, the odds are minuscule that our definition will gain dominance. It would surely be recognized widely in an association test administered at random, but the key words in it would most rarely be offered in response to the stimulus word "productivity."

Handicapped from the start, our definition is being muscled aside with discovery of the word by the media, the speechwriter, the itinerant consultant, and the grant-seeker. This discovery has a

---

14. See Craig-Harris article and Davis book cited in preceding footnote.

15. The dictionary synonym of "productiveness" or "capability of production" can be traced back to Quesnay and the Physiocrats, but the word *produktivitaet* was already used by Marx and Sombart in the sense of labor productivity in the 19th century. Our professional concept was certainly familiar to U.S. pioneers like C.D. Wright, who flourished in the 1880s and 1890s, although the word did not become established in our country until the 1920s.

telling centrifugal effect, multiplying connotations and helping to confuse what productivity is with conditions influencing it, with methods of raising it, and with positive or negative attitudes toward it. Ironically, managers, engineers, businessmen, and even professors have added to the confusion in their own zeal to heighten productivity consciousness and to encourage a quickening of the pace. They, too, on occasion misapply the word to other indicia of individual and organizational performance or misidentify the word with circumstances favorable to improvement.

Should one care about the dispersion of meanings of "productivity?" Yes, for the same reason that a patient would like to know if the doctor means "cancer" when he says "tumor." Science is not advanced by folklore. Truth is not established by a democracy of usage. Knowledge thrives on the obstinate insistence, in William James' phrase, that Tweedledum is not Tweedledee. Our position does not mean, however, that productivity in our sense cannot be raised by actions taken to raise it in some other sense. For decisionmaking, teaching and learning, communication, evaluation, and many other behaviors, however, it is useful to have a standard to which to aspire and from which to discern deviations.

To underscore what productivity is *not,* we cite a few examples. The purpose of so doing is not to disparage or debate but to illustrate the prevalence of semantic casualness and to provide a case for settling on a standard definition (like ours, of course).

A survey conducted in the fall of 1972 by Louis Harris and Associates[16] provides striking evidence of the meaning of "increased productivity" to the public at large and to people in particular occupational and income groups. Eighteen different answers (including "Don't know") were offered by 1,578 persons "questioned at their homes," but only two showed any (and only weak) kinship to the preferred professional definition: "Same number of people produce more" and "More output in the same

---

16. The figures cited in this paragraph and the next appear in *Second Annual Report,* National Commission on Productivity, Washington, March 1973, p. 86.

amount of time." The first answer was given by 10 percent of all respondents, and the second by 8 percent, while 18 percent acknowledged that they "Don't know;" but all the percentages add to more than 100 (actually, to 124), so some respondents ventured more than one opinion. College-educated respondents were somewhat more familiar with the idea of productivity, but still showed impressive ignorance; 15 percent gave the first answer and 9 percent gave the second, while another 9 percent "Don't know" (the sum for the 18 replies is 128 percent). The pattern for professional respondents is similar, but the number of multiple answers is greater (the percentage total is 138); 13 percent gave the first answer, 11 percent gave the second, while 9 percent "Don't know." Executives, too, seem overwhelmingly unaware of the meaning of productivity; 15 percent offered the first reply, and 10 percent gave the second, while 13 percent "Don't know" (the total percentage is 127).

More remarkable is the fact that the dominant answer given by respondents is "More production, more products made." This reply confuses productivity with its numerator. Over a quarter of all respondents, 28 percent, shared this erroneous view. A similar percentage, 27, is reported for executives. College-educated and professional respondents were less informed; 33 and 31 percent, respectively, thought that productivity meant production.

Three comments are in order, two of which hark back to earlier statements. First, if it were "logical" to conform to popular confusion and equate production and productivity, we should still need a word for productivity (especially for the connotation here preferred). Second, popular understanding or misunderstanding cannot define the proper foci of scholarly concern. After all, economists and others *are* interested in productivity as well as production. Third, and more significant, is the likelihood that revealed ignorance concerning productivity is not exceptional. What should specialists expect a poll to show if the affective or target word were, say, "money," "credit," "capital," "depreciation," "inflation," "tax reform," or "recession?" This rhetorical question hardly counsels complacency; it warns all torchbearers that they may be marching in the middle of larger competing fires.[17]

Unfortunately, the voluminous contemporary literature that deals with productivity contains enough confusion to seem to authorize lax usage elsewhere. Like the layman answering the pollster, a writer with credentials is often capable of maintaining a more or less precise idea of productivity and at the same time treating it as an "okay word" to be laden with a freight of fantasy. A 1978 textbook, for example, defines a "productivity index" as a ratio of "output obtained" to "input expenditure," but goes on to relabel the numerator "effectiveness" and the denominator "efficiency." Obviously, one okay word deserves two others, but which two? Thus, a 1974 article by two professors proclaims the equation "productivity = job enrichment + quality of worklife." A little bit of diligence would surely unearth articles that just as validly equate "productivity" with, say, "money + management;" or, still better, with "morale + money + management." At a 1976 conference, the head of a productivity institute averred, however, that "productivity is an attitude that says all work can be done better by continuous application of creative thinking, problem solving and energetic job performance." Here is a hero sandwich containing still other approved goodies. Additional illustrations of hyperbole could be cited, but the point is sufficiently clear.

Concluding this chapter, we note that many ratios that do not meet the quantity criterion (in whole or in part) are commonly called "productivity." This label may be used wittingly, as in at least one painstaking interestablishment study of value added (in dollar terms) per production-worker man-hour in many manufacturing industries.[18] It may be used less wittingly, as seems to be

---

17. Joan Robinson, longtime first lady of the economics profession, has made a pertinent remark worth mentioning here: "Economic concepts such as wealth, output, income and capital are no easier to define precisely than the wind. Nevertheless, these concepts are useful, and economic problems can be discussed." (*The Accumulation of Capital,* 2nd Edition, Macmillan, London, 1966, ix.)

18. Benjamin Klotz, Rey Madoo, and Reed Hansen, "A Study of High and Low 'Labor Productivity' Establishments in U.S. Manufacturing," scheduled to appear in *New Developments in Productivity Measurement,* University of Chicago Press, Chicago, 1980, with a comment by I.H. Siegel.

the case in a number of companies that have set up bonus systems under the Scanlon Plan: payrolls and output are compared without adjustment for price change through time in both numerator and denominator. The productivity label is frequently misassigned also to accounting-based money ratios in the business community, now that "productivity" has become an "in" word.

The misuse of the word need not cause mischief, but it also *can,* just as taking an unprescribed or wrong pill. For this reason, an Appendix Note 5 is included on the Scanlon-Plan and value-added ratios. Non-productivity ratios are certainly useful; and they can even contribute to the raising of productivity. Their nature should be clear to the user, however, who must be on guard against erratic changes and misinterpretation. As a memorable advertising slogan for an unremembered product once observed, "it is fun to be fooled, but it is more fun to know."

Chapter 4
How To Set Up A Company Measurement Program

From the *why* (Chapter 2) and *what* (Chapter 3) of company productivity measurement, we proceed to the *how*—the ways in which a company may seek to implement its decision to monitor performance. The discussion that follows is based on a meager literature,[1] experience in consultation, and information shared by company officials. Circumstances and needs differ, of course, from company to company, so the guidance here offered has to be adapted to particular cases. After some general remarks, plausible company procedures are considered under eight heads:

1. The decision to measure
2. The task force and its charter
3. Program information and communication
4. Inventory of data resources and skills
5. Auxiliaries: consultants, liaison officers, trainees

---

1. Some company case studies pertaining to productivity-improvement programs in general include ideas applicable to productivity measurement in particular. See reports cited in Chapter 2, footnotes 10 and 11; also see Bruce Lepisto, "A 'Market Basket' Approach to Air Force Logistics Command Depot Maintenance Productivity Measurement," *Productivity Enhancement in Logistical Systems,* U.S. Department of Commerce, May 1975, pp. 119-35.

6. Design of measurement system
7. Installation and "debugging"
8. Instructions for operation and recommendations for evolution

General Considerations

Size is itself an important determinant of a company's aims in monitoring, of the scope and detail of the undertaking, and of the way in which the company proceeds to implement the measurement decision. A small company will not require so formal a system as will a larger one. Nor will it have to organize so explicitly, or take so long a time, for design, installation, and "debugging" of a system. A larger company, on the other hand, is much more likely to possess the technical expertise, financial and computing capability, and managerial competence for detailed or sophisticated measurement and analysis. A larger company with facilities at more than one location may wish to set up a pilot program and test it before replication. Similarly, a company with multiple divisions may develop unevenly in its perception of a monitoring need, and one division may take the lead as the others lag or do not follow at all. Indeed, even though we speak of *company* programs, we may really mean programs for divisions or other major company components that are mostly self-governing.

A system is more easily developed and installed at companies that have a measurement tradition. Productivity monitoring is more likely to appear the logical next step where special studies have frequently been made beyond the routine requirements of the accounting and budgeting cycles and where work measurement has already been practiced to some degree. Even in such receptive companies, however, progress toward monitoring may be far from tranquil; managers of extant control systems may feel threatened by the advent of a new one, and rumor mills may flourish in the absence of an effective information campaign. Still worse, successful inauguration of a measurement system does not assure its institutionalization; measurement is not certain to continue as a vital and evolutionary tool of management under self-renewing leadership. Experience shows that enthusiasm often flags and vision fades as innovators leave the scene and bequeath their achievements to the care of epigones.

Although a company ought to have a "grand design" of its eventual measurement system in view, it may be wise to proceed modestly, by stages, according to its priorities and current resources. In monitoring, to attempt too much too soon is surely as hazardous as to do too little too late. As has already been suggested in this monograph, even an incomplete system or one that has obvious technical limitations can make a constructive contribution to a company's rate of productivity growth.

In developing its program, a company with limited in-house talent may do well to call on outside consultants. Such supplementation of resident technical resources could reduce the number of false moves, shorten the time required for design, and yield a more authoritative result. On the other hand, a system has to be a company's "own," and responsibility for it cannot be delegated to others by contract. After the consultant leaves, a company has to keep a turnkey system viable and operational with internal staff.

For some companies that are interested in the benefits of measurement, monitoring need not, of course, be the logical next step. In their situation, the trinity of survival, autonomy, and profitability could best be served, perhaps, by something as material and immediate as cash. Measurement is not a first aid. For the wrong companies, to give primacy to formal monitoring would be as digressive as picking daisies in a battlefield.

Decision to Measure

"Topside wants it:" this phrase makes the difference between measurement as a tool and measurement as a toy. The importance of commitment, sponsorship, and support on the part of appropriate "higher-ups" cannot be exaggerated—especially if, as is typically the case, the impetus to measure does not originate with them. In the current economic setting, however, they may be inclined to follow a fashion, take an explicit interest in productivity, and entertain proposals to monitor performance in the interest of improving it.

Typically, experimental measurement begins at a lower echelon or at a field station, where it is practiced voluntarily and obscurely by, say, a serious manager, statistician, engineer, operations analyst, or "misassigned" econometrician. This local idea can acquire company-level recognition and significance only if it is "sold" to, "discovered" by, or appropriated by a cognizant official of central office or headquarters. An idea that thus flies upward from line to staff comes back down with the imprimatur of authority.

Preferably, when the front office approves of the notion of designing and installing a measurement system, it should have a fairly precise view of company needs and of time and cost limits. It should prescribe guidelines in accordance therewith, but not the specifics. The latter should be left to the chosen instrument for implementing the decision.

Task Force and Charter

The chosen instrument for design and installation of the system ought to be an *ad hoc* group of company employees that signals its "clout" by its composition. This task force, steering committee, or council should be chartered to represent company leadership in the development of a suitable system consistent with the prescribed guidelines. It should have an interdisciplinary working corps of different quantitative skills recruited from strategic company departments or facilities. In addition, it needs members with symbolic credentials, such as honorific titles or known closeness to top officials.

In attempting to translate its mandate into a measurement system, a task force may either (a) find it feasible to devise a monitoring scheme that satisfies the company need and meets the stated time and cost constraints; or (b) decide that amendment is desirable in some important aspect. In the latter case, the task force should seek early renegotiation of its charter with regard to the scope or scale of the anticipated system, the time required, or the cost entailed. Revision of expectations is better than disappointment of them. Another confidence-retaining approach is to make delivery according to the original charter, indicate feasible and desirable improvements, and recommend development of a second-generation model while the first one is used.

Information and Communication

From the very beginning of its existence, the task force should take the initiative to advertise its constructive intent. Spelling out its mission, it should spread the word to lower management and the operating staff that no revolutionary "new order" impends. It should establish communications with a labor union or labor-management committee if either is already on the scene. It should take advantage of company newspapers or other in-house media to tell its story. Another challenge to the task force is to convince managers of extant control systems to cooperate—to assure them that the introduction of productivity measurement is not part of an arcane, imperial plan of some rival faction.

The task force may invoke two other tactics if extensive cooperation in the measurement process is required at all levels of organization. One is to designate "productivity officers" throughout the company; these may be middle-level and lower-level managers or persons selected by them. The officers would continue their regular work at their usual sites, but would have a liaison function, assisting two-way communication. The other way of selling the system as it develops is to conduct briefings, seminars, and dry-run demonstrations.

Data and Skill Resources

A major undertaking preparatory to design of the measurement system is to make a methodical survey of the company's data and skill resources. The review should cover existing data bases, routine printouts of the "management information system," earlier special studies and analyses, and current and past programs of work measurement. Such a review often occasions surprising discoveries—of "private" or local data caches, primitive quasi-productivity measures, prior initiatives that failed of fruition or diffusion, and isolated enclaves of knowledgeable but underutilized personnel. It may be politic for the task force to recognize such harbingers, precedents, or pioneers in the language or technical details of the new measurement system.[2]

Auxiliaries to Task Force

Outside consultants may be required in addition to resident productivity officers for expeditious accomplishment of the task force's mission. A consultant working with rolled-up sleeves like a member of the measurement team is far more useful than a white-glove academic kibitzer or a prestigious hit-and-run expert. He should be required to do much more than give "canned" advice. He should tailor prescriptions and formulas to fit the needs, constraints, data supply, etc. of the company that has engaged him.

The more detail required in the measurement system, the greater will be the reliance of the task force on the liaison services of the productivity officers. By virtue of location, these officers already have or could obtain needed information on subproducts and subactivities down to the work or cost centers.

Another incidental function of the task force that cannot be slighted is to assure that a sufficiently trained resident staff is on hand to operate and maintain the measurement system after it is installed. The task force is able to perform some of this training, having "learned by doing" and from reading and consultation.

---

2. G.E. Sadler, now of the American Productivity Center, reports that few production managers and engineers seem to be aware that the comptrollers of their companies regularly supply productivity-related data on Form MA-100 in the Annual Survey of Manufactures. With better in-house communication, the completed form or the underlying factory records could be exploited more effectively in a company measurement program. About 70 thousand manufacturing establishments annually submit this form to the Bureau of the Census.

The briefings, seminars, and dry-run demonstrations already mentioned could be used as training vehicles. The productivity officers also are being trained by their association with the project; they constitute valuable "cadre" for the post-development period.

Designing the System

The chief obligation of the task force is to arrive at a first-generation monitoring system that satisfies company needs and constraints as set forth in the original or amended charge. "First-generation" suggests that the system will be evolutionary; the same word and "amended" further suggest that the task force will, if desirable or necessary on the basis of its learning experience, make timely request for alteration of the charter terms. Codification of major changes, especially in the time schedule or budgeted costs, is important for avoidance of disappointment at the top and below.

As its work progresses, the task force will discover for itself the significance of some of the brief comments made earlier in this monograph. It will encounter data gaps and try to get around them—or, instead, decide that some subgoals should be deferred and others given higher priority. It will perceive targets of opportunity that tempt digression for the company's greater good. It will become curious as to the practical consequences of choosing one concept or procedure rather than another. It will acquire respect for the difference between verbal and literal algebra.

For a little more concreteness, we indicate some of the challenges that the task force will face, either to accept or reject. In making a companywide productivity measure, it may wish to compare one that is based on deflated sales with another based on weighted end products and with a third based on subproducts that "add up" to end products and are also representative of an exhaustive list of broadly defined subactivities. It may have an inspiration for devising an unrequired measure for a subactivity known to be a bottleneck or otherwise critical to profitability. It may wish to test the implications of alternative weighting schemes, or of different approaches to measurement of the quantity of capital.[3] It may wish to examine the possibilities afforded by the data system for deriving a price form of the productivity index as well as the more conventional quantity form that receives most attention in this book.

Installation and "Debugging"

Actions of the task force apart from actual design should have paved the way for initiation of measurement on a trial basis and for routine operation of the system by others after a "shakedown" or "debugging" period, which may last several months. These actions, already mentioned, include: the discovery of in-house sources of appropriate data; the dissemination of information intended to encourage understanding, cooperation, and receptiveness at all staff levels; the prepositioning of liaison officers; and the conduct of a minimal indoctrination and training program.

The task force remains in charge during the shakedown period, and the consultant should still be available, even if ties have been loosened. Trial operation of the system should disclose needs for different data, for revision of techniques, or for modification of administrative procedures. It should also give clues to the drafting of instructions for compilation and processing of data—and to the improvement of the system in the next phase. Afterthoughts are often the best; after one finds *a* way of doing something, *the* way could occur to him.

Instructions and Recommendations

Before the task force is disbanded, and preferably with the avuncular oversight of the consultant, an instruction manual has to be written for guidance of operators of the system and for help-

3. The idea of "inflation accounting," discussed for at least a generation, has finally been embraced by the Financial Accounting Standards Board for corporate annual reports beginning 1979. As companies experiment with the idea, it may become easier to make credible measures of real capital for productivity measurement. See "Inflation Accounting," *Business Week,* October 15, 1979, 68ff.; *Journal of Commerce,* October 5, 1979; or the report cited in footnote 11 of the preceding chapter.

ing them to make the system their own. The manual should have at least two parts. The first should disclose the nature of the system, its structure, data sources and methods, and uses of the results. The second part should concentrate on the measurement process itself and procedures for carrying it out—on data acquisition and processing, periodicity, forms and reports, and staffing.

The final act of the task force, perhaps, is to make delivery of early results of the measurement system with a copy of the manual and with recommendations for use of the numbers and for continuing evolution of the system. On the basis of the knowledge it has gained, the task force is in a good position to suggest how the numbers may effectively be analyzed and applied, how they may assist production, how they may contribute to a constructive labor-management dialogue, and how the measurement system may be coordinated with other management tools already used or contemplated. Especially important is the task force's written view of the future—of the next phase in measurement, of needs for improvement that are already visible, and of ways to accommodate probable growth or change with respect to company structure, product lines, and markets.

Chapter 5
Examples of Company Productivity Measurement

To assist companies that may be interested in measuring their own productivity, this chapter offers some examples of what other companies are doing or have done. These examples were disclosed in a brief survey of accessible published and unpublished materials. Additional information is obtainable from the cited publications, companies, and compiling organizations.

Wide Variety

The examples cover a wide range of industries and productivity denominators. They include transportation, distribution, and other services in addition to manufacturing. They take cognizance of the expanding efforts being made to measure productivity in the public sector. As has already been stated in this monograph, these efforts have a spillover effect in the private sector, where measurement of the output of services (and of construction) in "physical" terms on a subproduct basis has lagged and where a Chinese wall has too long separated "productivity measurement" and "work measurement." The examples include productivity indicators for capital and intermediate input as well as labor, and for composite factors (labor and capital) and all inputs (factor and intermediate) combined.

55

No example was found of systematic use of the price form of the productivity definition. After the quantity form becomes more familiar to the business world, the merits of the price form should gain increasing attention. The latter form is more congenial to the traditional concern of accounting with costs and prices and to the recurrent public and private concern with the wage-price-productivity connection in the economics of inflation (see Appendix Note 1).

Compilations of Cases: Private Sector

A rarity of the literature—a short book on company productivity measurement published in the 1960s by The Conference Board[1]—provides six case studies. Two of these, for General Oil Company and International Business Machines Corporation, refer to labor productivity. Two, for Johnson & Johnson and an unnamed producer of durable goods ("a large, multiplant manufacturer of a variety of complex products"), refer to capital as well as labor. Two others—for a "division" of a medium-size manufacturer of machinery and equipment and a "large manufacturing company" located in "Mideast" United States—refer to intermediate as well as factor (labor and capital) inputs.

Descriptions of the measures used by the six companies reveal an unsurprising diversity of data and methods. With respect to output, two companies weight physical quantities of products; two others deflate sales; and two estimate real value added, one by the application of an in-house measure of subproduct cost to labor expense plus overhead charges, and the other by separate price deflation of gross-output value and of subtracted intermediate-consumption value. Two references are made to adjustment for changing composition of output—by the usual method of "chaining" in one case and by the probably superior, though

---

1. J.W. Kendrick and Daniel Creamer, *Measuring Company Productivity,* The Conference Board, New York, 1965, is a reprint of the 1961 edition with minor corrections and the addition of a (sixth) case study.

"subjective," method of introducing hypothetical base-period weights for new products in the second case.

The input measures also vary considerably. Man-hours, actual or paid-for, appear in weighted or unweighted form; and, in one instance, they are estimated by deflation of total compensation by an index of adjusted hourly rates of pay. Fixed capital is estimated gross or net; and revaluation in base-period prices is accomplished, as usual, with patience, some ingenuity, and the aid of more or less relevant price indicators. In one case, capital input is estimated as a sum of equivalent man-hours. Value figures for working capital are converted into "quantities" by price deflation; and intermediate inputs are also estimated in real terms by deflation of money values rather than directly by the weighting of physical quantities.

The American Productivity Center, a nonprofit organization based in Houston, has also compiled some case studies for presentation in its brief intensive course on company productivity measurement. The cases include: the "common staffing study" of the International Business Machines Corporation; the company-wide labor and capital productivity-monitoring system of a "major insurance company," which apparently depends heavily on work measurement; the labor-productivity program of Detroit Edison; a "decentralized" manufacturer's emerging program, which began with sales per employee, has converted to labor-weighted output per direct-labor hour, and also is tentatively using output dollars per square foot as a measure of capital productivity; a productivity-monitoring system at Phillips Petroleum, constructed for the company from measures selected by operational managers; a comprehensive monthly monitoring effort of United Airlines explicitly seeking to raise productivity by measuring it with respect to labor, capital, and energy; and a system of plantwide productivity monitoring used by General Foods in setting cost-reduction targets for its farflung facilities.

The "common staffing study" mentioned above was described at a seminar of the U.S. Department of Commerce on company productivity measurement held in New York in February 1976.

This initiative of the International Business Machines Corporation aims at increasing the productivity of its non-manufacturing employees. Begun in 1968, this program complements the productivity-monitoring system for manufacturing adopted a decade earlier. It covers "non-touch" labor in 34 plants located in 13 countries. The scheme requires computation, tracking, and comparison of quasi-productivity ratios for 160 "activities" common to all plants.[2]

The National Center for Productivity and Quality of Working Life, a federal creature that expired at the end of September 1978, also contributed, with its predecessors, to enlargement of the library of current cases. In one of its publications,[3] it described the programs for productivity improvement launched by five companies—including Detroit Edison, an example used by the American Productivity Center. The other four companies are Beech Aircraft, Honeywell, Thiem, and U.S. Steel. No explicit reference was made to the role of measurement, if any, in the improvement programs of the latter two.[4]

A companywide monitoring effort was launched at Detroit Edison under the aegis of its president in 1972, with chief emphasis placed on "accountability" and "responsibility" at or below the departmental level. By October 1974, 80 percent of the employees, including those engaged in engineering and construction activities, were covered by work-measurement procedures intended to

---

2. *Commerce America,* March 29, 1976, p. 17.

3. *Improving Productivity: A Description of Selected Company Programs,* National Center for Productivity and Quality of Working Life, Washington, December 1975.

4. Since the discussion of the Thiem program mentions a profit-sharing plan, the company may make use of some sort of proxy for productivity numbers. The writeup for U.S. Steel features establishment of labor-management committees at the company's plants and use of "intensive communications" to personalize the need for productivity improvement. From the viewpoint of this monograph, the film used in the promotional campaign misses an opportunity to propagate a correct productivity definition—a common fault of "P.R." films and opinion surveys (such as the Harris poll cited in Chapter 3). The U.S. Steel film tells workers that "you can make it [the word 'productivity'] mean whatever you want it to mean." Indeed, "improved productivity doesn't necessarily mean bigger output by fewer people. It simply means that what we turn out will be better than what the other guy turns out." Apart from spreading confusion, this kind of fuzzy statement helps to reinforce the presumed suspicion concerning "productivity" that the film is intended to allay.

discern underperformance and overstaffing and to provide the basis for corrective action. It is not clear that a comprehensive labor-productivity index is computed for the company; but, with so detailed and broad a measurement system in place, a "bottom-up" summary based on weighted subproducts should be easy to devise. On the other hand, the detailed measures seem to satisfy a clear management need, and they yield benefits that ought to show up positively in any labor-productivity indicator devised for the company as a whole.

At Beechcraft, improvement in a measure of "equivalent pounds of airframe manufactured ready for delivery per payroll dollar" was adopted in 1972 as the criterion for an incentive-pay plan. The plan was extended in 1973 to include friendly competition among "teams" of five or more workers. This program is closely tied to another, which aims at "zero defects." Additional formal efforts have been made at the company to raise productivity and reduce costs—through work simplification, employee suggestions, value engineering (to achieve desired functional capability at least cost), materials conservation, and emphasis on "commonality" in product design, engineering, tooling, work layout, and actual production.

With leadership from the very top, Honeywell instituted a productivity improvement program in 1973 that aimed especially at white-collar areas—"sales, engineering, clerical, and administrative departments." It emphasized job enrichment for employee motivation. Although productivity is correctly defined as the "relationship between the quantity of goods and services produced and the quantity of resources required," the measure used for the company as a whole is "the ratio of sales to pay" (including fringe benefits), neither the numerator nor denominator being deflated. Each of the 20 company divisions operates as a separate profit center, and each department is encouraged to adopt whatever measure it wishes that "directly relates input of resources to output." The department head is responsible for performance and is expected to take the remedial action that he and his supervisors deem to be warranted by a review of the measures. In 1974, the company adopted a special program to determine "time per task" of office and technical groups engaged in repetitive work having tangible outputs.

Another report of the National Center for Productivity and Quality of Working Life (NCPQWL), published in 1976, gave considerable attention to company measurement.[5] One paper in this report refers to a measure of output per man-hour used in the Mill Products Division of Aluminum Company of America since 1968 for comparison against industry performance. The individual products in the numerator are weighted by unit cost.[6]

Another paper in the same report deals with productivity measures devised for grocery warehouses by the National-American Wholesale Grocers Association. The system was begun over 30 years ago, and it now provides "23 different productivity ratios for each . . . department in the warehouse." These ratios refer to tons per man-hour in functions performed by direct labor, repack labor, indirect labor, and support labor. Each warehouse's results can be compared with industry and subindustry averages for the same period. The author of the paper points to the common confusion between the cost ratios of accounting and performance ratios, such as productivity: "When warehouse labor percent to sales goes up, management feels concern. But it may, in fact, be totally unrelated to productivity."[7]

The National Productivity Center has also prepared several reports dealing with the Scanlon Plan,[8] which features the use of a quasi-productivity ratio for bonus payments to employees. The "base ratio," a norm reflecting past experience, relates total labor

5. *Improving Productivity Through Industry and Company Measurement,* National Center for Productivity and Quality of Working Life, Washington, October 1976.

6. M.E. Gantz, Jr., "Productivity Measurement at Alcoa." *ibid.,* 37-44. Another discussion of the Alcoa program by Gantz appears in the U.S. Department of Commerce's *Situation Report,* Productivity Series, Bulletin 4, August 1975.

7. G.E. Peck, "Measurement of Warehousing Productivity," in report cited in footnote 5, pp. 46-57. The quotation appears on p. 48.

8. The NCPQWL reports include: *A Plant-Wide Productivity Plan in Action: Three Years of Experience with the Scanlon Plan,* May 1975; *Recent Initiatives in Labor-Management Cooperation,* February 1976; and *Recent Initiatives in Labor-Management Cooperation, Volume II,* Spring 1978.

cost to the market value of net sales. The sales term excludes defective returns; it often represents the value of production—when sales are actually adjusted for the change in inventories of finished goods and goods in process. Changes in the ratio of labor cost to sales do not necessarily indicate improvements in true productivity, as the remark quoted in the preceding paragraph has already noted. Scanlon companies, however, could avoid fooling themselves by computing true productivity indicators based on "physical" quantities; and at least one showcase company (DeSoto) does so, in addition to computing unit labor cost with and without bonus pay. Among other companies with Scanlon Plan experience are Midland-Ross, Parker Pen, and Dana. Despite the purist position of this monograph on definition, it is a demonstrable fact that trying to measure productivity, even crudely, can enhance productivity consciousness throughout a company and thereby help raise company productivity.

The determined campaign of the 1970s to apply and improve productivity measurement in federal facilities has entailed, among other things, a continuing review of private cases. This review has been conducted by, or under the leadership of, the Joint Financial Management Improvement Program (JFMIP), an interagency venture authorized by the Budget and Accounting Procedures Act of 1950. A conference cosponsored by JFMIP and the National Center for Productivity and Quality of Working Life in 1976 provided the occasion for presentation of papers on the improvement efforts made at Xerox (Education Division) and at Travelers Insurance—as well as at two other companies already mentioned here, Detroit Edison and Honeywell. In all four cases, measures are used for monitoring subactivities, and all these measures have labor denominators.[9]

The JFMIP annual report for fiscal year 1974 includes descriptions of the DeSoto Scanlon Plan (mentioned earlier) and the Texas Instruments productivity effort. The latter company obviously has a measure of "physical output per man-year," and

---

9. *Implementing a Productivity Program: Points to Consider,* Joint Financial Management Improvement Program, Washington, March 1977.

it also makes use of a current-dollar measure of net sales per unit of payroll cost.[10]

In 1972, another illustrative report concerning private improvement efforts was published—this one by the U.S. Army Management Engineering Training Agency. The report is based on interviews of personnel at 12 "well-managed companies . . . to determine the systems and methods they use to measure and improve productivity in their organization." All the companies had work-measurement systems in place. One (a bank) showed an interest in broadening the monitored subactivities, and three also had rough productivity measures for the company as a whole (a major steel producer, a maker and distributor of footwear, and a manufacturer and seller of electronics equipment).[11]

Additional Cases: Private Sector

Scholarly journals, management and business magazines, daily newspapers, and miscellaneous other publications offer additional evidence of company use of actual or so-called productivity measures to support pursuit of survivability, autonomy, and profitability. A few examples are cited in this section, with neither claim nor illusion of near-exhaustiveness.

First, we mention three case studies reported in scholarly business-oriented periodicals. One, based on a doctoral dissertation, examines the course of physical output per man-hour in the St. Paul and Tacoma Lumber Company in 1903-38. It considers changes in component mills and major activities as well as the record for the firm as a whole; and it also compares the company trend against a similarly constructed industry measure.[12] The

---

10. *Productivity Programs in the Federal Government, FY 1974, Annual Report to the President and the Congress, Joint Financial Management Improvement Program, Volume Two: Case Studies,* Chapters 3 and 6.

11. *Survey of Productivity Measurement Systems in Non-Government Organizations,* U.S. Army Management Engineering Training Agency, Rock Island, May 1972. This publication was partially financed by the National Commission on Productivity, a predecessor of the National Center for Productivity and Quality of Working Life.

12. W.R. Sherrard, "Labor Productivity for the Firm: A Case Study," *Quarterly Review of Economics and Business,* Spring 1967, pp. 49-61.

second study, pertaining to Eli Lilly, a large pharmaceutical manufacturer, shows real value added per man-hour, per unit of capital input (equipment, structures, and inventories), and per unit of labor and capital combined in the interval 1963-72. The methodology is patiently described, and an extra feature is the computation of a variant capital-productivity measure that treats research and development expenditure as a "capitalized" input.[13] The third study is still broader in scope, showing deflated output per unit of deflated input of labor, capital, materials, etc. for a "large, multiplant" producer of automobile and truck components in 1968-71. Capital input is estimated as "service value" of fixed assets, cash, accounts receivable, inventory, etc. More specifically, this input is calculated as a sum of annuity (or perpetuity) values that take account of each asset's base-year cost and productive life and of the company's cost of money.[14]

Three more examples are presented as a unit because they echo the grocery-warehouse case already presented. In 1951, in the same publication that carried an account of the Lever Brothers & Unilever program of in-plant and interplant productivity measurement, an engineer of Shell Oil described a study intended to raise efficiency in the warehousing phase of petroleum-products distribution. This study not only provided the usual sort of informatic.. ᴜn times required for the accomplishment of various tasks but also showed something that has acquired greater interest over the years—the number of gallons of gasoline and of lubricating oil "moved" through different company depots per unit of "paper work."[15] A second example is a study of productivity made by a doctoral candidate in 1975 with support from an arm of the National Association of Wholesaler-Distributors. It shows how a firm might go about tracking its own real

13. D.L. Cocks, "The Measurement of Total Factor Productivity for a Large U.S. Manufacturing Corporation," *Business Economics,* September 1974, pp. 7-20.

14. C.E. Craig and R.C. Harris, "Total Productivity Measurement at the Firm Level," *Sloan Management Review,* Spring 1973, pp. 13-29.

15. S.S. Tomlin, "Productivity Standards—Warehousing," *Advanced Management,* March 1951, pp. 19-22. The article on Lever Brothers is cited in Chapter 2, footnote 4.

sales, adjusted for gross-margin changes, per man-hour.[16] In 1977, a study of labor productivity was being made at Harvard Graduate School of Business Administration for 60 different supermarket tasks in 100 product categories. Output was measured, not in sales or margins, but in "standard hours."[17]

Many companies contributed speakers on their own systems of productivity measurement to the seminar program initiated by the Department of Commerce in 1975. Among the companies so participating and not yet mentioned in this monograph are American Express, Eastman Kodak, Fisher Scientific, Westinghouse, and Western Electric. The Westinghouse tracking system apparently evolved out of static work measurement.[18] Western Electric has a long tradition in work measurement; but, in the 1960s, a need became evident for global corporate measure, so company indexes of real value added per unit of labor, capital, and the two factors combined were devised. At a Department of Commerce seminar in 1976, a spokesman for Western Electric showed additional measures that referred to intermediate input and to composite intermediate and factor input.[19]

Our survey continues with a distillation of information obtained from accumulated newspaper and magazine clippings relating to productivity. They suggest that the experience of unrelenting inflation since the middle 1960s has encouraged companies to seek measurable control of cost pressures by: (a) raising white-collar

---

16. Stephen Skancke, *Productivity in Wholesale Distribution,* Distribution Research & Education Foundation, Washington, No Date.

17. This study, by H.S. Takeuchi, is described briefly in *Business Week,* March 7, 1977, p. 55.

18. James Wearn, "Productivity Monitoring and Measurement," *Situation Report* (U.S. Department of Commerce), Productivity Series, Bulletin 5, August 1975.

19. Based on notes taken at the 1976 seminar held at Seton Hall University; and on a press release by The Conference Board on remarks made by V.A. Dwyer at a presentation in New York on May 23, 1973, "Management Uses of Productivity Measures."

Incidentally, an unpublished paper presented in November 1951 before a public-private panel on productivity measurement by R.W. Burgess suggests that Western Electric already had (as did Lever Brothers and Unilever) a sophisticated program of work measurement. The title of the paper was "Integration of Productivity Studies with the Operating and Accounting Statistics of Industry."

productivity through application of work measurement; (b) raising worker productivity in general via "psychological" and other techniques not requiring heavy investment; (c) raising capital productivity through modernization of plant rather than large-scale replacement; and (d) raising energy productivity through conservation and process improvement. In the illustrative material that follows, companies are cited that appear to have measurement programs or to have set quantitative targets for their efforts.

Consultants report a considerable emphasis on work measurement in offices that have "high-volume, repetitive" jobs. Time standards are being used for budgeting, work scheduling, worker assignment, and procedural improvement. Static "efficiency" computations seem to be favored; but the advantages of broader monitoring—of larger subactivities and of groups of workers rather than individuals—are being discovered, and tracking through time is certain to be adopted also by more of the firms that start with traditional work measurement. It would be a mistake to assume, of course, that office workers like to be measured and that the measurement criteria always capture the essence of a job. Incentive pay sometimes compensates for the uneasiness also engendered. Substantial numerical savings are reported for Aerospace Corp., Winters National Bank & Trust, and Northwestern Life Insurance. Aetna, Government Employees Insurance, Chase-Manhattan Bank, First National City Bank, Bank of Maryland, and National Bank of North America are among the organizations that were using clerical work measurement by 1970.[20]

Companies that monitor worker performance closely are recognizing the need for profit-sharing arrangements, improved two-way communication, job-retraining and transfer opportunities to offset job loss in reorganization, and "positive reinforcement" by rapid promotion or substantial pay increase. Most large companies—Ford, General Electric, Weyerhaeuser, Warner-Lambert, American Telephone & Telegraph, Goodrich,

20. *Business Week,* November 14, 1970, pp. 54ff.; *Wall Street Journal,* August 7, 1979.

etc.—have "behavior-modification" programs, and many others that know nothing of B.F. Skinner's psychology practice similar techniques as naturally as Molière's gentleman spoke prose. Pitney-Bowes places great emphasis on internal communication as well as profit-sharing. Motorola and Firestone are among the companies examining the merits of worker participation for productivity increase. Such companies as Herman Miller, which have long records in worker participation in management and profit-sharing, are viewed with new and growing interest.[21]

In many industries, companies are taking the expedient of "rounding out" existing facilities to increase capital productivity rather than embarking on huge programs of investment in more modern "greenfield" plants. The cost of money, the time required for new construction, environmental and other governmental regulations, the risks of litigation, and uncertain profitability in the face of foreign competition oblige many industrialists to cope rather than to dare. The steel, aluminum, chemical, paper, and oil-refining industries are courting the danger of worse future obsolescence as they try to raise the performance of existing establishments. The nation may well face a serious threat of entropy of enterprise, but it is also good to learn, for example, that "squeezing more out of existing equipment" has positive short-run payoff in the steel industry: "Such prodding resulted in the fine-tuning of a 19-year-old furnace at J&L's Cleveland Works that has boosted monthly production to 70,000 tons from a rated capacity of 25,000 tons."[22]

Many companies are cooperating through their trade associations in the voluntary energy-conservation program of the Department of Energy, and they are also investing in computerized systems of energy management to cut the cost of lighting, heating, refrigeration, air-conditioning, and processing. Shopwell reported in 1978 the achievement of a 25-percent

21. *Journal of Commerce,* April 18, 1978; *Business Week,* January 23, 1978; *Wall Street Journal,* August 9, 1973; and *New York Times,* October 1, 1976.

22. *Business Week,* December 18, 1978, p. 77. See also *Wall Street Journal,* June 11, 1979, and *New York Times,* June 18, 1979.

reduction in utility cost in two New York stores with the aid of a computerized system; it expected to install the system in 34 of its supermarkets by the end of the year and in 68 by the end of 1979.[23] Celanese Corporation has sought to increase its energy productivity, as well as its labor productivity, to withstand the rising cost of power and petroleum-based feedstocks. Energy consumption per pound of product was reported in 1978 to have been reduced by 32 percent since 1972. A further reduction of almost 3 percent was accomplished in 1978 "by installing energy-efficient equipment and processes." In 1977, the company reported a striking gain of 10 percent in labor productivity—far greater than the national rate or the rate of its chief competitors.[24]

In accordance with Section 373 of the Energy Policy and Conservation Act of 1975, the larger companies located in the "10 most energy-consumptive manufacturing industries" are reporting their energy productivity directly to a federal agency. They have targets for improvement, and their progress is tracked. Although separate company figures are not published, some of the narrative reports of companies on steps taken to improve energy efficiency have been released. A few hints of numerical savings are contained in such reports for December 1977-January 1978 concerning Alcoa, Beatrice Foods, Campbell Soup, General Mills, General Motors, Gulf Oil, and Agrico.[25]

Since "much of the wasted energy in this country is lost before it ever gets out of the electric generating plant," considerable attention has been directed toward improvement of performance in individual stations and systems. Downtime, or poor capital productivity in particular, is a matter of concern in large coal-fired plants as well as in nuclear facilities. To encourage a better record of plant "availability," on which productivity depends, it has

23. *Journal of Commerce,* April 4, 1978. See also *Washington Post,* August 3, 1979, on District of Columbia business plans to meet specific industry conservation targets for department stores, restaurants, groceries, printing, etc.

24. *Business Week,* October 8, 1979, pp. 121-22; and *Journal of Commerce,* April 13, 1978.

25. U.S. Department of Energy, *Annual Report on Industrial Energy Improvement Program,* Volumes I and II, June 1978.

been proposed that statistics be published regularly on the comparative performance of utilities. These statistics might, for example, list the 10 "best" and 10 "worst" powerplants and systems.[26]

Federal Examples

Two kinds of labor-productivity measures are used to assist management in the federal agencies, which are the analogues of private companies. First, "atomic" measures are constructed for work centers or other small units of organization for control of operations and for budgetary purposes. These are the indicators of primary concern to the Office of Management and Budget. A second approach is taken by the U.S. Bureau of Labor Statistics, which prepares agency measures from agency data referring to output of "final" or end products. These measures are not published, but "functional" consolidations, which cut across agency lines, are.

The two approaches are not so incompatible as is conventionally supposed, even in the professional literature. All final or end products can either (a) be viewed as the subproducts of specific terminal subactivities or (b) be broken down into subproducts corresponding to the many subactivities performed in an organization. The latter subproducts—or a "representative" selection of them—may be combined with suitable labor-requirement weights into correct measures of final products (virtually self-adjusted, moreover, for changes in inventories of uncompleted products). Accordingly, it is possible in principle, without confusion and without duplication, to develop a hierarchical set of measures from the lowest levels of organization up to the agency as a whole. (Whether agency output is measured on a final-product or subproduct basis, a consolidated measure for federal government as a "conglomerate" contains duplication to the extent that one agency consumes the final output of another.)

---

26. *Commerce America,* December 5, 1977, p. 12. Also of interest is the report of an inconclusive symposium on *Public Utility Productivity: Management and Measurement,* New York State Department of Public Service, Albany, August 1975.

The Social Security Administration and the Defense Supply Agency are examples of federal organizations that could use their extensive work-measurement systems for construction of articulated aggregates of subproducts.[27]

It is instructive, especially for the measurement of productivity of services in the private sector, to peruse a list of "activities" and "output indicators" compiled by the Bureau of Labor Statistics in the course of making its consolidations for "functions." In 1976, for example, a computer printout for 25 of the 28 functions covered by the Bureau required 168 pages. In this list, by way of further illustration, the "mission" of the Social Security Administration with regard to the function called "citizens' records" entailed 47 activities and output indicators; and the National Transportation Safety Board's duties with respect to "regulation—inspection and enforcement" translated into 39 activities and output indicators.[28]

State and Local Governments

During the past decade, the growth of government employment and outlays below the federal level has also engendered explicit interest in productivity improvement and measurement. The efforts of the states of Washington and Wisconsin and of cities such as New York have received considerable publicity.

Many federal agencies have contributed funds for research in addition to sharing experience and sponsoring conferences. For example, the National Science Foundation has made research awards for measuring productivity in administrative services, such as budgeting and management analysis in state governments, purchasing by state and local governments, personnel manage-

---

27. See Chapter 8, on the Social Security Administration performance measures, in the report of the Joint Financial Management Improvement Program cited in footnote 10; and M.H. Baker, "Productivity Management in the Defense Supply Agency," *Public Administration Review,* November-December 1972, pp. 771-76.

28. *Productivity Programs in the Federal Government, Supplement to Volume I: The Measurement Data Base,* Joint Financial Management Improvement Program, Washington, July 1976.

ment in cities of different size, inspection and quality control, and computing and information services. It has supported research of the Urban Institute on "a comprehensive measurement system for reporting on the productivity of the principal services delivered by cities." This Institute, a non-profit organization, has developed measurement recommendations for such areas as local transportation, solid-waste collection and disposal, policing, water supply, handling of citizen complaints, and library service.[29] Another example of federal stimulus to local productivity monitoring was the sponsorship by predecessors of the National Center for Productivity and Quality of Working Life of reports on the applicability of work measurement to municipal management—a tool apparently used effectively to raise productivity in Phoenix, Arizona and Riverside, California.[30]

Some Foreign Examples

In reconstructing their war-shattered economies, European countries and Japan laid great stress on methods and measurements of productivity improvement. The unstinting technical aid supplied by the United States needs no recounting here. Suffice it to say that the Bureau of Labor Statistics program of direct reporting of unit man-hour requirements by companies had enormous influence and served as a model for imitation. The European Productivity Agency, set up in 1953 as a branch of the Organization for European Economic Cooperation (which itself came into being in 1948), energetically propagated information on

29. See Chapter 7, on state and local government productivity, in the report of the Joint Financial Management Improvement Program cited in footnote 10; R.O. Mason, "Research in Productivity Measurement at the National Science Foundation," in *Improving Productivity through Industry and Company Measurement,* pp. 69-73; and *Proceedings of the Grantees' Conference on Research on Productivity Measurement Systems for Administrative Services,* Arizona State University, Tempe, 1976.

30. *Improving Municipal Productivity: Work Measurement for Better Management,* National Commission on Productivity and Work Quality, Washington, November 1975; and H.P. Hatry and D.M. Fisk, *Improving Productivity and Productivity Measurement in Local Governments,* National Commission on Productivity, Washington, June 1971. For a non-federal report on the same general topic, see *Improving Productivity in State and Local Government,* Committee for Economic Development, New York, 1976.

methods and results of measurement at the company and plant levels. It used a periodical, *Productivity Measurement Review,* as the chief vehicle for reporting new research; and it also published a memorable report on time trends and interplant comparisons of unit labor requirements.[31] This show of interest in company-level measurement has continued to the present day in the work of the European Association of National Productivity Centers (Japan is a member) and of individual scholars. As in the United States, physical output per man-hour or per worker has to be supplemented by weaker reflectors of productivity based on sales and value added.[32]

This chapter concludes with a notice of the impressive and inexpensive, yet "personalized," program of productivity assistance to companies that is being conducted by the Canadian government. The original intent was to help participating firms to diagnose their structures and operations with explicit reference to productivity, but it soon became evident that greater cooperation would be obtained by expansion of the analysis to bear on profitability. Government representatives examine a wide array of financial ratios, quasi-productivity ratios, and physical-productivity figures (if any); compare these figures with those of unidentified "competitors;" provide confidential reports on strengths and weaknesses; suggest remedial actions; and make follow-up visits. Among the "productivity" ratios included in the company reviews and interfirm comparisons are value added per

---

31. *Productivity Measurement, Volume II: Plant Level Measurements—Methods and Results,* Organization for European Economic Cooperation, Paris, January 1956.

Among the American contributions to *Productivity Measurement Review* that are pertinent to this chapter is an article by D.E. O'Connell, "Subproduct Measurement of Production and Productivity," May 1959, pp. 47-49. O'Connell reported use of the subproduct approach in studies of a paint factory and a corrugated-box plant.

32. See, for example, C.F. Pratten, *Labour Productivity Differentials within International Companies,* Cambridge University Press, London, 1976; and another book by the same author, *A Comparison of the Performance of Swedish and U.K. Companies,* Cambridge University Press, London, 1976.

An up-to-date summary of "interfirm productivity comparisons" and related investigations in various countries is presented in the December 1979 issue of *Integrator,* the house organ of the European Association of National Productivity Centers: "Measuring Corporate Productivity," pp. 43-60.

production-worker hour and value added per square foot of floor area. In some instances, rough measures based on unweighted quantities are also available, like "pounds of metal cast per unit of energy or the numbers of pairs of pants per yard of material."[33]

Coda

The Canadian experience recalls several of the themes that have animated this book. Productivity is vital to the survivability, autonomy, and profitability of private firms. Efforts to measure company productivity and to compare it to that of other organizations can contribute signally to the upgrading of performance. Even unsophisticated productivity measures, partial productivity indicators (confined, say, to labor), and proxy ratios that in some sense relate desired benefits to incurred costs can be used with constructive effect. Careful analysis and interpretation of the numbers, with due regard to the literal algebra of their derivation, can compensate in some degree for their limitations.

But this book also emphasizes other points that a company should consider in the design and conduct of a program to meet its special monitoring needs. More than research interest may be found, for example, in the comments offered on the subproduct approach, its blending with end-product measurement, the convergence of work measurement and productivity measurement, the meaningful quantification of capital, the use of energy consumption as a surrogate for capital services, responsible deflation, and extension of traditional accounting to include the price form of productivity. There is also practical content in the observations made on top-level commitment and support, coordination with other extant managerial systems, employee communication, and use of the numbers fairly and for

---

33. Imre Bernolak, "Enhancement of Productivity through Interfirm Comparisons," in *Improving Productivity through Industry and Company Measurement,* pp. 59-65. More recently, in October 1979, Bernolak presented two other informative papers on the Canadian program at a London meeting sponsored by the European Association of National Productivity Centers and the British Council of Productivity Associations: "Development and Issues of Interfirm Comparisons in Canada" and "The Measurement of Outputs and Capital Inputs."

labor-management dialogue. Above all, productivity monitoring is commended to companies in this book for service as a tool to upgrade performance rather than as a statistical toy.

Appendix Notes

Appendix Note 1

Quantity and Price Forms of a Productivity Index

Defining productivity as output quantity ÷ input quantity, we may, according to verbal algebra, rewrite this ratio as output value/output price ÷ input value/input price. If the two value figures are set equal to each other, they "cancel out," and we have productivity equal to input price ÷ output price. Furthermore, if we confine value to payrolls and use man-hours as the quantity of input, productivity becomes both output per man-hour (the quantity form) and average hourly earnings ÷ unit labor cost (the price form).

So much for verbal algebra. Proceeding to literal algebra, we may translate the equation, average hourly earnings = unit labor cost x output per man-hour, into a consistent set of index numbers for the corresponding variables, thus:

$$\frac{\Sigma c_i \pi_i}{\Sigma c_o \pi_o} = \frac{\Sigma c_i \pi_o}{\Sigma c_o \pi_o} \cdot \frac{\Sigma c_i \pi_i}{\Sigma c_i \pi_o}.$$

Here, $c_i \pi_i$ and $c_o \pi_o$ refer to average hourly earnings corresponding to individual products, c_i and c_o refer to unit labor costs for individual products, and π_i and π_o refer to output per man-hour for individual products. The productivity index, which is of the so-called Paasche variety, is, by construction, the quotient of an index of hourly earnings and a so-called Laspeyres index of unit labor cost. If productivity were represented instead by a Laspeyres index, $\Sigma c_o \pi_i / \Sigma c_o \pi_o$, the companion index of unit labor cost would be of the Paasche variety. All indexes are written above as ratios of weighted aggregates, but they may also be converted easily into weighted internal averages of relatives (π_i / π_o's in the case of productivity, etc.).

We may start from more elaborate verbal identities and again arrive at literally equivalent quantity and price forms of a

77

productivity index. For example, writing payrolls in these two ways:

payrolls = unit labor cost x output per man-hour x man-hours

payrolls = output x unit labor requirements
x average hourly earnings,

we have "templates" for writing the corresponding index numbers. More than one compatible set of indexes is obtainable. It is easy to show that

$$\frac{\Sigma c_o \pi_i m_i}{\Sigma c_o \pi_o m_i},$$

one of the derivable quantity forms suggested by the first identity for payrolls, is equal to

$$\frac{\Sigma q_i r_o e_o}{\Sigma q_i r_i e_o},$$

one of the reciprocals of unit labor requirements indicated by the second identity; and that both, in turn, are equal to ratios of certain indexes of average hourly earnings and unit labor cost. Similar statements can be made about

$$\frac{\Sigma c_i \pi_i m_o}{\Sigma c_i \pi_o m_o} \quad \text{and} \quad \frac{\Sigma q_o r_o e_i}{\Sigma q_o r_i e_i}.$$

Again, these indexes may be re-expressed as weighted internal means of productivity relatives.

In discussions of "wage inflation," it is commonly asserted that a rise of x percent in hourly earnings (including fringe benefits) minus an expected gain of y percent in man-hour productivity spells an advance of (x - y) percent in prices. This statement is an approximation that (a) involves the price form of productivity and (b) assumes a perfect correlation between increases in unit labor cost and prices. Thus, starting with the price form, $e_o = c_o \pi_o$, and perturbing all the variables, we get $e_o + \Delta e = (c_o + \Delta c)(\pi_o + \Delta \pi)$, which works out to

$$\frac{\Delta e}{e_o} \doteq \frac{\Delta c}{c_o} + \frac{\Delta \pi}{\pi_o} + \frac{\Delta c \, \Delta \pi}{c_o \pi_o}.$$

For sufficiently small increments, the rightmost fraction becomes negligibly small, and we obtain this approximation:

$$\frac{\Delta c}{c_0} \doteq \frac{\Delta e}{e_0} - \frac{\Delta \pi}{\pi_0} \, .$$

Analogous relations are derivable for small changes in index numbers.

When the percentage change shown by an index of productivity is expressed as a difference between two quantity or price indexes, it has to be remembered that (1) the statement is inexact and more correct for infinitesimals than for discrete displacements; (2) the form and content of the actual aggregates involved are mathematically relevant, despite a common neglect in the pseudo-calculus of index numbers; and (3) accounting identities have to be preserved in any interval of perturbation. Furthermore, approximations that are patiently worked out (by incrementation followed by suppression of second-order and higher differences) may be surprisingly unlike the expressions that seem intuitively obvious.

A company may wish to explore the practical advantages of making a productivity index by continually "chaining" short (Laspeyres, Paasche, or other) "links." To do so requires no embrace of theoretical rationalizations involving logarithmic differentiation and unconstructible Divisia indexes. An accessible introductory discussion appears in R.G.D. Allen, *Index Numbers in Theory and Practice,* Aldine, Chicago, 1975, Chapter 5.

Appendix Note 2

Labor-Productivity Indexes that are Internal Averages of Productivity Relatives

A typical measure of labor productivity relates a Laspeyres price-weighted index of output to an unweighted index of man-hours:

$$\frac{\Sigma p_o q_i}{\Sigma p_o q_o} \bigg/ \frac{\Sigma r_i q_i}{\Sigma r_o q_o}.$$

If the quantities of individual products are weighted instead by unit man-hour requirements of the base period, the productivity index condenses to the BLS-WPA form,

$$\frac{\Sigma r_o q_i}{\Sigma r_o q_o} \bigg/ \frac{\Sigma r_i q_i}{\Sigma r_o q_o} = \frac{\Sigma r_o q_i}{\Sigma r_i q_i},$$

which is also expressible as a weighted internal average of productivity relatives ($r_o / r_i = \pi_i / \pi_o$):

$$\frac{\Sigma r_i q_i (r_o / r_i)}{\Sigma r_i q_i}.$$

Condensation is also achievable if the original output index is untouched while the man-hour relatives in the labor-input index are suitably weighted. Thus, we may write

$$\frac{\Sigma p_o q_i}{\Sigma p_o q_o} \bigg/ \frac{\Sigma p_o q_o (m_i / m_o)}{\Sigma p_o q_o} = \frac{\Sigma p_o q_i}{\Sigma p_o q_o (m_i / m_o)} = \frac{\Sigma p_o q_i}{\Sigma \left(\dfrac{p_o q_i}{r_o / r_i} \right)},$$

which is weighted harmonic mean of productivity relatives.

Tools for analyzing the difference between alternatively weighted productivity indexes are presented by I.H. Siegel in *Aggregation and Averaging,* The W.E. Upjohn Institute for Employment Research, May 1968, pp. 23-26; in other writings cited there; and in "Supermatrix Approach to Least-Squares Adjustment, *The American Statistician,* December 1968, pp. 22-23.

Appendix Note 3

Reconciliation of "Work Measurement" and "Productivity Measurement" on Subproduct Basis

If end products are suitably decomposed into their subproducts, we may write aggregate ratios of "standard hours to actual hours" for the base period (t_o) and a compared period (t_i) and derive productivity indexes of the kind considered in Appendix Note 2. The "standard" is a weight, a unit labor requirement for each subproduct. It may be an "engineering" or other estimate (r_x), a fixed "historical" standard (r_o), or a changing "historical" standard (r_i). If either of these historical standards is used, the derived productivity index condenses to an unequivocal internal mean of productivity relatives. The following table shows the pertinent algebra for the three different standards.

Standard	Ratio of Standard to Actual Hours for t_i	t_o	Productivity Index for t_i (base t_o)
r_x	$\dfrac{\Sigma r_x q_i}{\Sigma r_i q_i}$	$\dfrac{\Sigma r_x q_o}{\Sigma r_o q_o}$	$\dfrac{\Sigma r_x q_i}{\Sigma r_x q_o} \Big/ \dfrac{\Sigma r_i q_i}{\Sigma r_o q_o}$
r_o	$\dfrac{\Sigma r_o q_i}{\Sigma r_i q_i}$	$\dfrac{\Sigma r_o q_o}{\Sigma r_o q_o} = 1$	$\dfrac{\Sigma r_o q_i}{\Sigma r_i q_i}$
r_i	$\dfrac{\Sigma r_i q_i}{\Sigma r_i q_i} = 1$	$\dfrac{\Sigma r_i q_o}{\Sigma r_o q_o}$	$\dfrac{\Sigma r_o q_o}{\Sigma r_i q_o}$

Appendix Note 4

Real Value Added and Composite-Factor Productivity

If the aggregates for gross output and intermediate inputs can be adequately expressed in constant dollars of the base period, we have this Laspeyres index of real value added:

$$\frac{\Sigma p_o q_i - \Sigma P_o Q_i}{\Sigma p_o q_o - \Sigma P_o Q_o}.$$

A second summation symbol, S, may be introduced into this expression if the intermediate inputs assignable to each end product are combinable into subaggregates:

$$\frac{\Sigma p_o q_i - \Sigma S P_o Q_i}{\Sigma p_o q_o - \Sigma S P_o Q_o}.$$

A condensed index of composite-factor productivity is obtained if such a measure of real value added is divided by a measure of composite factor input (say, for labor and capital) that corresponds exactly to the numerator in scope and that also has base-period weights. Thus, if we precombine portions of the factor inputs assignable to specific end products, we have:

$$\frac{\Sigma p_o q_i - \Sigma S P_o Q_i}{\Sigma p_o q_o - \Sigma S P_o Q_o} \div \frac{\Sigma S w_o f_i}{\Sigma S w_o f_o} = \frac{\Sigma p_o q_i - \Sigma S P_o Q_i}{\Sigma S w_o f_i}.$$

As a condensed index, this productivity measure is guaranteed to be an internal mean of productivity relatives if the net output corresponding to every end product is positive (or zero). Here is a rearranged form that is a weighted arithmetic mean:

$$\frac{\Sigma \left[S w_o f_i \left(\frac{p_o q_i - S P_o Q_i}{S w_o f_i} \right) \right]}{\Sigma S w_o f_i}.$$

Note that $(p_o q_i - S P_o Q_i) \div S w_o f_i$ is indeed a net productivity relative; it is really divided by $(p_o q_o - S P_o Q_o) \div S w_o f_o$, which happens to be equal to 1.

Appendix Note 5

Relation of Dollar Ratios to Productivity

Without demeaning the usefulness of ratios like *value added per man-hour,* we need to be aware that they are not productivity ratios, either of the "quantity" form or the "price" form. In interpreting them, we should consider what verbal algebra says: value added/man-hours = (value added/output) x (output/man-hours). Thus, only if value added per unit of output (or unit value added) is constant from plant to plant or from firm to firm can value added per man-hour be regarded as equivalent to a "physical" productivity ratio. This sort of stabilization of the price element is not feasible in practice. Incidentally, the verbal identity also shows that, if appropriate data were available, the quantity form of productivity could be made equal to a price form: value added per man-hour (an input price) ÷ unit value added (an output price).

The ratio of *dollar sales to payroll dollars* (or the reciprocal) is also not a true productivity ratio even though the Scanlon Plan amicably uses such figures for making bonus payments. Indeed, physical output per man-hour may change significantly from one year to the next while the payroll percentage of sales dollars remains constant. Verbal algebra tells us that: sales value ÷ payrolls = (price x quantity) ÷ (average hourly earnings x man-hours). Thus, the Scanlon-type ratio equals physical productivity times a ratio of product price to hourly pay. Only if the latter ratio (the reciprocal of a price-form productivity indicator!) is constant does the sales/payroll dollar ratio correctly show the change in physical productivity.

It is fitting that the last statement in this note and this book should offer two disclaimers: (1) no "sexist" insensitivity is meant to be evidenced by non-avoidance of the traditional term, "man-hours;" and (2) references to the Scanlon Plan are not meant to slight other companywide incentive systems based on the sales/payroll ratio. (See B.L. Metzger, "Productivity Improvement through Profit Sharing," *Manufacturing Productivity Frontiers,* January 1980, pp. 1-10.)

DATE DUE

DEC 16 1991			
DEC 11 1990			
DEC 11 1991			